DATE DUE

MY 11 '99			
JY 21 99			
NO 2 9 '99			
AP 5 '00			
DE 19 '01			
NO 2 '06			

DEMCO 38-296

LAND OF THE
TIGER

LAND OF THE
TIGER

A NATURAL HISTORY OF THE INDIAN SUBCONTINENT

VALMIK THAPAR

UNIVERSITY OF CALIFORNIA PRESS

BERKELEY   LOS ANGELES

I dedicate this book to some of the people I have met and closely worked with who have committed their lives to saving this fragile land of the tiger:

Firstly to my original 'Tiger Guru' Fateh Singh Rathore. Then to S.Deb Roy, Bittu Sahgal, Brijendra Singh, Ullas Karanth, Billy Arjan Singh, Joanna Van Gruisen, Peter Lawton, Chris Jordan, Dave Currey, Ajit Sonakia, P.K.Sen, Peter Jackson, G.S.Rathore, Raghunandan Singh Chundawat, A.K.Barua, Toby Sinclair, Ashok Kumar, Divyabhanusinh, Avininder Singh, Vikram Soni, Geoff Ward, the Tiger Link network that has responded so rapidly to the plight of the tiger, and to all those forest guards, foresters and rangers that I have met in my travels across India, the true trench soldiers of wildlife who roam night and day to desperately save the rapidly vanishing land of the tiger.

Finally to Paola Manfredi who in the last twelve years has been a great inspiration to me.

FRONTISPIECE *A tiger in the ruins of the garden palace at Ranthambhore*
PAGE 6 *Portrait of a tiger*

This book accompanies the TV series *Land of the Tiger*, produced by the BBC Natural History Unit, Bristol, and first broadcast in 1997.
Series producer: Mike Birkhead.
Producers: Pelham Aldrich-Blake, Mike Birkhead, Martin Hughes-Games

© Valmik Thapar 1997
Valmik Thapar has asserted his right to be identified as the author of this work in accordance with the Copyright Designs and Patents Act 1996

General editor: Caroline Taggart
Designed by Rachel Hardman Carter
Picture research by Frances Abraham
Maps by Line & Line

University of California Press,
Berkeley and Los Angeles, California
Published by arrangement with BBC Books,
an imprint of BBC Worldwide Publishing
ISBN 0 520 21470 6

Jacket printed by Lawrence Allen Limited,
Weston-super-Mare.
Colour separations by Radstock Reproductions, Midsomer Norton.
Printed and bound in Great Britain by Butler & Tanner Limited,
Frome and London

9 8 7 6 5 4 3 2 1

CONTENTS

ACKNOWLEDGEMENTS

WRITING A BOOK and keeping it linked to a film is no easy task, particularly when it must be written in snatched periods between location filming. Under any circumstances, however, it would be difficult to do justice to a subject that even a lifetime is not enough to absorb. The experience has nonetheless been a remarkable learning process about the land of the tiger and its rich diversity of life. Filming took me to places of which I had previously only heard, and some of them remain indelibly etched in my mind. Sadly, I also witnessed the tragedy that is engulfing the wildlife of the subcontinent. We are involved in a race against time to save it.

Fifty years after the Independence struggle, the moment has come to base new political movements around the protection of our natural heritage. Without this we will enter an era of human disasters, losing the health and quality of our lives to short-term and mindless economic development. And while this happens the wilderness will vanish forever. We must join forces around the world to save some of the magnificent natural spectacles that still survive, and battle with those intent on their destruction. I hope this book helps to convince people that this a cause worth fighting for.

I have many people to thank for their help and encouragement while I was writing this book: Mike Birkhead, the producer-director of the television series; Sheila Ableman, Martha Caute and Trish Burgess for their advice and editorial input to the manuscript; E. Gough for information about snakes; Pelham Aldridge-Blake and Vanessa Berlowitz for the information and assistance they provided; Dr Wendy Darke for not just information but teaching me to snorkel in the Lakshwadeep Islands; Shanthi K for the Topslip encounters; Kanchan and Sidhrajsinh for their Kutch hospitality; Anna and Philip for their London hospitality; Amanda Taylor for all inputs; special thanks to Toby Sinclair for his kind help in so many different ways; Kunjumon P.C. for his computer assistance with the text and Sunny Philip for his help in the office.

I must acknowledge some of the remarkable wildlife biologists of this country: Dr Ullas Karanth for reading parts of the text and giving me his valuable comments; Dr Ragunandan Singh Chundawat for his suggestions about portions of the 'high altitude text'; Dr R.Sukumar's work on elephants; Dr Ajith Kumar's work on lion tail macaques; Dr Ravi Chellam's work on the Asiatic lion; Dr Asad Rahmani's work on the great Indian bustard and so much more; Dr B.C. Chowdhury's work on the olive Ridley turtles; Ravi Sankaran's work on the Andaman and Nicobar Islands; Dr M.K.Ranjitsinh's work on the black buck; Dr Ishwar Prakash's work on the desert; Dr A.J.T.John Singh's work on wild dogs, and the work of a host of others in creating an ever-expanding reservoir of information on the wilderness of our country.

Finally, the most vital link in the chain has been Paola Manfredi, who stood solidly with me, helped with the text, commented on the manuscript and, during the stress of filming and writing, was always around for me to lean on. To her I am eternally grateful.

VALMIK THAPAR
New Delhi, 1997

7

KARAKORAM

HINDU KUSH

Kunjerab

NORTHWEST
FRONTIER
PROVINCE

Dachigam

JAMMU & KASHMIR

Hemis

Islamabad ●

AFGHANISTAN

Srinagar ●

HIMACHAL PRADESH

HIM

Lahore ●

Pin Valley

PUNJAB

Govind Sagar

Valley of Flower

Sutlej

PUNJAB

Kedarnath

Nanda Devi

Lal Suhanra

NE

HARYANA

Corbett

Indus

THAR DESERT

Delhi ■

Ganges

Dudhwa

Bardia

PAKISTAN

Kath

BALUCHISTAN

RAJASTHAN

Sariska

UTTAR PRADESH

Desert National Park

Keoladeo Ghana (Bharatpur

Lucknow ●

Ranthambhore

Chambal

Shivpuri

Kirthar

SIND

Panna

Karachi ●

Lake Kinhar

Bandhavgarh

P.

MADHYA PRADESH

Little Rann

Satpura

Nal Sarovar

Narmada

Bori

Kanha

Marine

Melghat

Pench

GUJARAT

Velavadar

Tadoba

Sat

Gir

MAHARASHTRA

Godavari

Mumbai (Bombay) ●

Godavari

INDIA

ANDHRA PRADESH

WESTERN GHATS

Arabian Sea

Nagarjunasagar

Koll

EASTERN GHATS

Krishna

Dandeli

GOA

KARNATAKA

Bangalore ●

Madra

Nagarahole

Vedanthan

Bandipur

Mudumalai

TAMIL NADU

LAKSHADWEEP
ISLANDS

KERALA

Cauvery

Point Cal

Cochin ●

Periyar

Wilpattu

S

Colombo ●

Horton Plains

REPUBLIC OF
MALDIVES

The external boundary of India,
as depicted here and on other
maps in this book, may not be
authentic or exact.

Indi

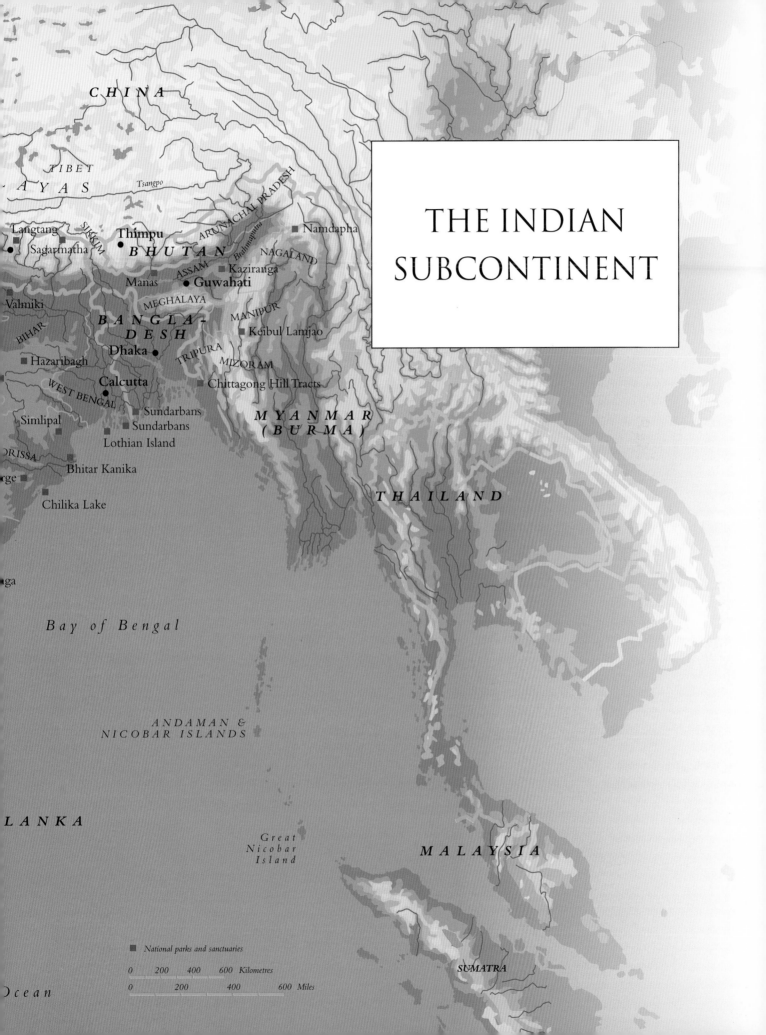

THE INDIAN
SUBCONTINENT

CHINA

TIBET

AYAS

Tsangpo

Langtang

Sagarmatha

SIKKIM

Thimpu

BHUTAN

ARUNACHAL PRADESH

Namdapha

Brahmaputra

NAGALAND

ASSAM

Kaziranga

Valmiki

Manas

Guwahati

MEGHALAYA

BANGLA-
DESH

MANIPUR

Keibul Lamjao

BIHAR

Dhaka

Hazaribagh

TRIPURA

MIZORAM

Calcutta

WEST BENGAL

Chittagong Hill Tracts

Simlipal

Sundarbans

MYANMAR
(BURMA)

Sundarbans

Lothian Island

ORISSA

Bhitar Kanika

rge

THAILAND

Chilika Lake

Bay of Bengal

ANDAMAN &
NICOBAR ISLANDS

aga

LANKA

*Great
Nicobar
Island*

MALAYSIA

■ *National parks and sanctuaries*

0   200   400   600 Kilometres

0   200   400   600 Miles

Ocean

SUMATRA

INTRODUCTION

At the end of the twentieth century, and after nearly fifty years of independence, the Indian subcontinent can still be justly proud of its enormously varied flora and fauna. In India alone, 13,000 species of flowering plants and 65,000 species of fauna have been recorded, including 2000 fish, 1200 birds and 340 mammals. There are numerous species of reptiles and amphibians, including turtles, crocodiles and over a hundred species of frogs and toads. India is also the only place in the world which boasts both lions and tigers – indeed, despite the country being steeped in tiger lore, the lion was the national animal until 1972.

This diversity of life is possible because of the wide variety of climates found on the subcontinent. In the northwest lies the great Thar Desert with an annual rainfall of less than 12 centimetres, while in the northeast Cherrapunji regularly receives more than 1060 centimetres. Temperatures in the desert can reach 50°C, while up in the Himalayas places such as the Dras valley in Kashmir have recorded temperatures as low as -45°C. A single place can also undergo great extremes: the town of Simla in northern India, for example, can experience zero humidity in December but 100 per cent in August and September.

If one expands the parameters to include the rest of the subcontinent the habitats become even more extreme, from the snowy heights of Nepal and Bhutan in the north to the genuinely tropical forests of Sri Lanka in the south; from the deserts of Pakistan in the west to the regularly flooded swamps of Bangladesh in the east. Even within the Himalayas there are distinct changes in vegetation: the sal trees of the foothills give way to oak, juniper, deodar, birch, pine, chestnut and others higher up, and parts of Ladakh are cold, sandy and stony deserts.

But while the extremes of climate and habitat explain the enormous diversity of life, they do not explain how this wealth of flora and fauna has managed to survive in

An eighteenth-century depiction of Lord Ganesha, the elephant god, wrapped in snakes, with his vehicle the mouse. Ganesha is worshipped by millions of people across the length and breadth of the Indian subcontinent; by association, this has probably helped the wild elephant to survive in many areas.

such an immensely crowded continent. For the wildlife shares its land – a total area of about 4.4 million square kilometres – with over 1.2 billion people. That is over 20 per cent of the world's population in about 3 per cent of its land area. The needs of the people put immense pressure on the habitat: whether it be the official damming of rivers that floods one area while parching another, the poaching of rhino for horn, elephants for ivory or tigers for bones, or the smaller-scale encroachment of villagers entering protected areas of forest in search of firewood or honey, wildlife and humans would appear to be in constant conflict.

It must also be remembered that wildlife legislation in India is very recent. Although a handful of national parks and game sanctuaries have existed since before independence, it was only in 1972 that the Wildlife Protection Act enforced new laws to prevent the flagrant abuse of India's wildlife. In the same year the Indian government launched Project Tiger, which aimed to set aside different habitats across the country in order to ensure the safety of the tiger. In the 1980s the Forest Conservation Act and the Environment Protection Act were initiated in an effort to strengthen existing legislation. India now has 560 protected areas, including 80 national parks, but much remains to be done if the natural life of India is to survive human depredation.

In Sri Lanka the first national parks were established in 1938, but in other parts of the subcontinent the concept of conservation is even younger than in India: Royal Manas Wildlife Sanctuary, the first in Bhutan, was created in 1966; and Nepal's 'flagship' Royal Chitwan National Park in Nepal dates only from 1973.

How, then, has it come about that such a wealth of wildlife has survived? That despite all the pressures, the diversity of both flora and fauna is the richest in the world? The answer lies, in part at least, in the special relationship that the people of the subcontinent have always had, and continue to have, with the other living creatures that share their land.

This special relationship is inextricably linked to religion. Despite the influx of cable television and Western consumerism, religion is still very important in rural life, though cultural change has started on a new generation and I fear that it will have a negative impact on the way we view wildlife. The Hindu concept of the sacred cow is familiar the world over, but Hinduism treats many other animals and birds with similar respect.

This was symbolized for me recently in Pench, in the heart of India, early one morning before the sun had risen. I was out tracking and found a fresh set of pugmarks which looked like those of a young tigress. As I followed the track, a group of quail rushed past me and in the distance I could hear langur monkeys alarm calling: the tiger could not be far away. For the next half an hour I followed the track, but slowly realized that the tiger had probably moved into thick forest to rest for the day. As

I turned a corner, I found a small shrine beside the road which the tigress had crossed. Looking more closely, I realized it was a shrine to Vaghadeva, the tiger god, and that someone had recently left offerings to the guardian of the forest. At one time such shrines were dotted across the subcontinent, as blessings from the tiger provided protection against evil.

Reverence for things natural also extends to trees and plants – in fact, tree worship is one of the oldest forms of religion in India. When travelling recently in the Satpura forests of central India, I came across a village whose people worshipped the local banyan tree as the most sacred site in the area. Such practices have led to the creation

Fig trees are sacred to many Indians and both the elephant god, Ganesha,
and the snake god, Naga, are worshipped around its formidable trunks and roots.

of 'sacred groves', areas which give complete protection to the flora and fauna within. The rules governing sacred groves are far stricter than those governing national parks, and even today, in the middle of nowhere, you may suddenly come across a sacred grove where 5, 10 or 20 hectares of dense forest reveal the traditional ability of people to protect all natural life.

And this attitude is not confined to Hindus. Buddhism, widely practised in the kingdom of Bhutan, also believes in protecting the natural world. Jainism bans the killing of any living creature, however small. This means that insects cannot be trodden on or involuntarily swallowed. Members of the Bishnoi sect will not burn wood until it is free of insect life, and will even sacrifice their own lives to protect trees and animals from poachers. In one instance a woman breast-fed a newborn deer until it reached maturity in order to save its life.

All these creeds – and to a lesser extent Muslims too – venerate certain creatures, celebrate them in festivals, propitiate them in prayers and do their best to protect them from harm. Central to all this, of course, is the tiger.

Tiger worship

Throughout its range, which once extended from Siberia to Southeast Asia, the tiger has been revered as the guardian of the forest. The tiger created rain and stopped years of drought so that people could grow food; kept nightmares away, guided young children on a path of safety and brought about healing. In areas of strong Islamic influence it was believed that Allah gave the tiger as protection to his followers and that anyone who transgressed the commands of Islam would be punished by the tiger.

Because of its large tiger population, India had many adherents to these beliefs, and Indian mythology is full of references to them. A legend from the northeastern state of Nagaland relates that the mother of the first spirit, of the first tiger and of the first man came out of the earth through a pangolin's den. Having the same 'mother', man and tiger are seen as brothers. In one part of northern Bengal the tiger god was worshipped by both Hindus and Muslims. Scroll paintings depict a Muslim holy man, carrying a string of prayer beads and a staff, astride a tiger and attacking all that was evil. In the area north of Bombay inhabited by the Warli tribes, paintings are still made that show the tiger as a natural part of life, sitting or walking through a village with a harmless, friendly look, very much as an undisturbed tiger would appear in reality.

The Warlis have always believed in the tiger god, Vaghadeva. There are carved wooden statues of the tiger all over their land, many of them phallic symbols, reflecting the tiger's importance as the bringer of fertility. Just before and during the festival of

*A Warli painting from Maharashtra reveals the striped image of the tiger
which governs so many facets of traditional Warli life even today.*

Diwali, when the earth is producing new plants in the harvested fields, the young
people sing and dance in a trance-like state to the music of a phallic-shaped instrument
called the *tarpa*. When the dancing is over, they worship Vaghadeva, commemorating
the most productive period of the year. Members of the village donate part of their
harvest profits to propitiate the tiger, whose statue is adorned with images of the sun,
moon, stars and trees, and possibly an entwined serpent – all symbols of life and its
endless regeneration. The Warlis regard the tiger as 'the greatest of all gods. The other
gods are there only because of him.'

Among the Warlis, the tiger's connection with fertility extends even to marriage
and pregnancy. Warli bridal couples wear red and yellow shawls resembling the skin of
the tiger when they visit the temple to propitiate Palaghata, the goddess of marriage.
Legend claims that if she is angry, the shawls will turn into a real tiger and devour the
couple. If this does not happen, the union is sanctified and the couple rendered fertile.

In the ancient Indus valley civilization, the supreme goddess, Durga, is always
depicted riding a tiger. Bringing light and peace to the Earth, Durga, whose name
means 'beyond reach', is the feminine force or *sakti*, created by the gods to combat the
evil male power that has percolated through the world. From her sprang the goddess

Preparing for the 'tiger dance' in Udipi in southern India.

Kali to join the fight, and the vehicle for this fight was the tiger. Why? Perhaps because man and tiger were said to share the same mother, but also perhaps because, as king of the forest, the tiger had power 'beyond reach' of any mortal. Even today, the image of Durga riding her tiger is omnipresent across India.

All along the south coast of India there is a tradition of tiger dancing that has its origins in religion but is nowadays more like a carnival than a sacred rite. The details vary from place to place, but one of the most exciting tiger dances to watch takes place in the small town of Udipi in the state of Karnataka in September. Although this coincides with celebrations to mark the Hindu Lord Krishna's birthday, it is thought that the dancing

LEFT *The goddess Durga riding her vehicle the tiger, which was regarded as the most powerful creature on land. Together the goddess and her vehicle could destroy evil and bring light on earth.*

This painting depicts Buddha offering his life to a starving tigress and her cubs so that they can live. This ultimate sacrifice reveals the entanglement of Buddhism and Nature.

may be Muslim in origin. Men of all ages paint themselves in stripes and don masks and tiger-like tails; in addition to ad hoc dancing in the streets there are competitions with prizes of money for the best dancers, and each year young children are initiated into the rituals of the tiger dance.

The tiger evokes myriad images: provider, protector, guardian and intermediary between heaven and earth. Tigers are depicted carrying princesses on their backs, growing wings in order to travel great distances to cure and heal, turning white to become part of the Milky Way and thus keep a protective eye on the Earth and its inhabitants, fighting dragons to create rain, guarding forests against thoughtless wood-cutters, changing into men and back again, carrying people into the next world, fighting evil so that mankind can love and reproduce. People have looked to them to prevent disaster, regenerate life and provide balance, peace and fertility. No other animal has so much attributed to it.

Airavata and Ganesha – the elephant gods

To Western eyes at least, the other enduring symbol of the subcontinent is the elephant. In Indian mythology, the milk-white elephant Airavata was produced when the oceans were churned and life created on this planet. Born out of water, it is a symbol for the source of all life, as well as motherhood, wealth, fertility and abundance. The elephant has long been associated with clouds and rain, and its presence regarded as auspicious.

Worship of the elephant god Ganesha (depicted as a human with the head of an elephant) dates back 2000 years and presumably originated in regions where elephants were numerous; his gentle nature has made him the most popular deity on the sub-continent. Every home, business and village in India has images and shrines to Ganesha, who is the god of the poor, credited with the ability to fulfil desires. Also the god of sagacity, he is believed to purify the mind and lend nobility to the goals of life. No activity, whether planting a tree, digging a well or building a house, must be done without invoking Ganesha, since he removes obstacles and promotes prosperity, peace and success. His festival, soon after the monsoon, is celebrated everywhere and involves submerging his image in water. I remember, when I was growing up in Bombay, seeing thousands of people gathered on Chowpati beach in celebration of the great elephant god – an awesome sight.

Equally awesome is Esala Perahera, a Buddhist festival held in Kandy in Sri Lanka, which centres around a tooth of the Buddha. This sacred relic, said to have been smuggled into Sri Lanka in the fourth century in the hair of a princess, is normally kept carefully

The religions of the subcontinent involve elephants, tigers, snakes and so much of the natural world. Here Vishnu, the Hindu god of creation, creates cosmic order by hauling up Sesha, the great cosmic serpent. Below, the turtle provides support.

guarded in a casket in a temple, but once a year, on the night of the full moon, it is brought out and paraded round the town amid much ritual, noise and celebration. The focal point of the celebration is a procession of some 130 magnificently adorned and bejewelled elephants. The principal elephant, treading a carpet of white cotton which is unrolled before him and preceded by saffron-robed monks, carries on his back a shrine containing the tooth.

Nowhere is the elephant held in greater esteem than in Kerala, in southwest India, where devotees are known as *ana kambakarans* – elephant maniacs. Every April people scour the state to find the thirty most magnificent tuskers to take part in the festival of Pooram. One elderly elephant at the temple of Guruvayurappan had long been the one honoured with the task of carrying the god's image throughout his three-day festival; when the elephant died Kerala went into mourning, cremating him with expensive sandalwood and making a full-length feature film of his life.

The monkey god

If Ganesha provides the strength to remove obstacles, the monkey god Hanuman provides the speed, agility and cunning to overcome them. The exploits of Hanuman are recounted in the epic *Ramayana,* compiled probably in the fifth century BC. According to this story, Hanuman went on a mission to the island of Lanka to rescue Lord Rama's stolen wife Sita. After locating her, Hanuman proved his loyalty to the doubtful Sita by opening his chest and displaying the names of King Rama, Sita and Rama's brother Lakshmana written on his heart. The king of Lanka, however, caught Hanuman and tied burning faggots to his tail. Undaunted, Hanuman raced around the kingdom of Lanka, setting it on fire, before dousing his flames in the Indian Ocean and then finally rescuing Sita and returning to India. Hanuman's victory against evil is the victory of the common man, so the monkey god is widely venerated.

Hanuman is endowed with magical powers which enable him to change shape, fly through the air and move mountains. In addition to symbolizing strength and cunning, he can bestow longevity on his followers and has the ability to transform powerful emotions into spiritual energy. He has the power to scare evil spirits, and his image, smeared with sacred oil and red ochre, is a common sight in countless villages. In some places he is even regarded as the giver of fertility and the provider of offspring. Such is Hanuman's importance that many temples and groves are dedicated to him, and hunting monkeys is taboo throughout Asia. The primate named after him – the Hanuman langur – is respected, fed and worshipped across India, and has thus survived the vagaries of time.

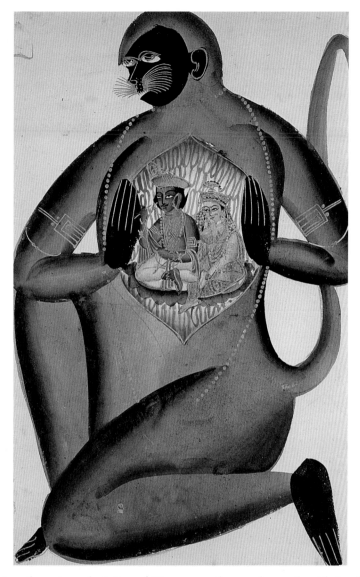

*A nineteenth-century depiction of Hanuman, the monkey god, with Lord Rama
and his wife Sita deep inside his heart. It was Hanuman who saved their lives
from the demons.*

At a temple in Delhi dedicated to Hanuman, *bahururipiyas* – impersonators of the
god – regularly dress up as monkeys, jump from the temple to the nearby trees, steal
fruit, leap on cars and generally behave in a riotous manner. What stronger proof could
one ask that animal worship is alive and well in India!

Reverence for monkeys has even allowed them to inhabit India's Central Secretariat
and Parliament House in Delhi. Every day troops of macaques roam the corridors of
power, causing havoc among administrators and snarling at ministers. Sometimes they

even tear apart the carefully chosen decor. Many special files have been started to deal with this nuisance, but some senior officers oppose moving the monkeys for religious reasons. Consequently, the macaques remain, growing in numbers and fed by the faithful for the blessings they bring.

Snake worship

The cobra family includes the monocled cobra and the king cobra, and these reptiles, with their puffed hoods, are the favourite subjects of snake worship, probably one of the most ancient cults in the world. In mythology the snake is the guardian of the Earth and its secrets, especially the secret of creation. Because of the strong phallic symbolism attached to snake worship, women play an unusually prominent role in many of the ceremonies.

The peacock dancers in south India celebrate the peacock's sacred role in rebirth and the unity of the cosmos.

In Hindu temples dedicated to Siva, the god of destruction and creation, the phallic *lingam* is often guarded by carved cobras, and there is usually a number of live resident snakes too. The serpent or *naga* guards the essence of life – water – and this is reflected in the image of the supreme god, Vishnu, embraced in giant cobra coils and protected by a seven-headed snake as he awaits the creation of life. Cobras are frequently found in paddy fields, where they eat rodents and other pests, so it is believed – with reason – that the presence of a cobra signifies a rich harvest to come.

Snake worship reaches its peak at the time of Nagapanchami, the festival of snakes, when the little village of Battis Shirala, not far from Bombay, has become famous for having the largest collection of venomous snakes in the world. A week before the festival, young men venture into the forests to 'persuade' the snakes to come out; they are then captured and kept in readiness. On the day of the feast people paint figures of serpents and birds on their walls. They then take a wisp of grass, tie it in the form of a snake and dip it into a prepared mixture of wheat and pulses. This, together with sweets and money, is offered to the live snakes. A cobra is paraded through the village, where the people worship it amid much merry-making. Women drop coloured incense on to the cobras' hoods. At sunset a procession of decorated bullock carts carries the snakes to the temple of Siva, where the ceremonies continue. Then the following day the men take the snakes back to the forest and release them where they found them.

Buddhism also embraces snake worship, and the *Jataka* tales in Buddhist literature claim that serpents gathered in the garden to help with the birth of Sidhartha, the Nepalese prince who became Buddha. Just as the *naga* guarded the sleeping Vishnu, so it protected Buddha while he slept near a well. Today a Buddhist snake charmer in Myanmar dances before a cobra's cave in an attempt to ensure the prompt arrival of the monsoons. Again, there is a logical reason for the cobra's association with the rains: young king cobras are born just before the monsoon, so their appearance is a harbinger of the life-giving rain to come.

The killer of snakes

The peacock's name in Sanskrit is *mayura,* which means 'killer of snakes', and carved images of peacocks with a snake in their talons are seen throughout India. Nor is this pure myth: peacocks carrying snakes have been observed in the wild. Peacock feathers are kept to ward off evil spirits, while burning feathers will cure snake bite. The peacock is generally believed to protect against cobras – it is said that its piercing cry is enough to addle snake eggs.

The peacock is very important in Hindu mythology, being the vehicle of the god Kartikeya, the god of war and all celestial armies, the cosmic mount of Kama, the god of love, and the sacred mount of Saraswati, the goddess of wisdom and poetry. In ancient India its wheel-like tail was a symbol of the all-seeing sun and all eternal cosmic cycles, but it also represents rebirth, the heavens and the stars, and the unity of the cosmos. Again, these beliefs are not confined to Hinduism – the peacock plays an important role in the Muslim story of creation.

The courtship dance of the peacock is the most glorious of all birds' displays because of the male's brilliant plumage. The tail feathers drop once the display is over, so various peoples, notably the Raj Gonds of Andhra Pradesh in Central India, collect them and make fantastic head-dresses for their own ceremonies. Troops of dancers go from village to village performing a sort of mock courtship in imitation of the peacock's dance, perpetuating its traditional link with fertility and regeneration.

Because of the reverence with which it is treated, the peacock has become common almost everywhere in the subcontinent, from the Himalayas to the forests of Sri Lanka, and is frequently found almost tame in villages.

The land of the tiger

Our journey through the subcontinent will explore the lives and habitats of these sacred creatures, and of many more of the thousands of species that make this such a richly diverse land. In the mountainous regions of the Himalayas, we travel through snow and ice to discover the hardy species that abound there. Here, among the mountain strongholds, the great rivers, the Ganges, Indus and Brahmaputra, are born, turning from tiny streams into raging torrents that sweep across the plains and down to the sea, creating some wonderfully rich and diverse habitats.

We take a sea voyage from India's eastern coast to the Andaman and Nicobar Islands, on to Sri Lanka and the little known Lakshadweep Islands, then up the western coast to the Gulf of Kutch in Gujarat, where the great desert of India begins. The desert, with its salt-flats and rolling sand dunes, stretches across the western flank of India to meet Pakistan. Here every drop of water counts and each year the eyes of the desert inhabitants scan the sky for signs of the monsoon. Elsewhere, the monsoon creates some of the wettest forest on the subcontinent, running down the western coast to the southernmost tip of India and into Sri Lanka: we will explore these too. Then our journey takes us back to the centre of India, home to those sacred species the tiger, the peacock, the langur and the cobra.

The land of the tiger continues to enthral me, providing the greatest pleasure and the sharpest pain. As the years roll by, forests decline, wildlife diminishes and the tragic consequences of careless human actions become more and more visible across the

This painting, which reveals the birth of the Ganges, was painted in Murshidabad, c.1760.
The river descends from Lord Siva's locks into a pool at his feet.

subcontinent. Nonetheless, parts of the area remain unspoiled and afford glimpses of magnificent animals and environments. I hope that by reading about some of the finest habitats and species in the world, people will come to see and understand the basic truth underlying the concept of the right to life.

Now let us start our journey. We begin high up in the mountains, for without them there would be little wildlife at all.

CHAPTER ONE

ICY
MOUNTAINS

I AM HURTLING OVER the Nepal Himalayas towards the highest peak in the world. I am in an old Russian helicopter that rattles and vibrates, at moments giving me the shivers. Suddenly my heart misses a beat. Peering out I see a glimpse of Mount Everest as it reaches for the sky. Within minutes the helicopter has landed in Syangpoche, 3500 metres above sea level within Sagarmatha National Park. The snow is piled up as I get out and confront the mountains. Time stands still and I am overcome by a sense of awe that has the magical power to silence. I am surrounded by peaks that rise around to heights of 6000 metres. Fresh snow clings to the slopes; I have never been so cold in my life. The air is thin and I can feel my heart beating as my blood pressure rises. The rugged beauty astounds me. No wonder these mountains were regarded as the abode of gods, saints and sages, places of meditation and learning. The legends of their origins are fascinating.

In the beginning, according to the epic *Mahabharata*, the god Vishnu lived on the northern shores of a great sea, his only companions a pair of seagulls. Each year the female gull laid her eggs close to the shore, but each year the sea swept in and washed the eggs away. The gulls cried to Vishnu for help. He opened his mouth and swallowed the sea, and in its place came Mother Earth. As Vishnu slept, exhausted by his bout of drinking, the demon Hiranyanksha leapt upon the Earth and ravished her with such violence that her limbs were thrown up into the sky.

The sacred mountain of Kanchenjunga, which means 'the five jewels of eternal snow', is said to be where the Tibetan god of wealth kept his treasures. Few mountain people would scale these peaks, as to do so would be sacrilegious. Beyond the Garhwal Himalayas towards the northeast rises a 6400-metre mountain called Kailash. This area is held as one of the most sacred for Hindus and Tibetan Buddhists. It is the abode and

The Machapuchare peak in the Annapurna region of central Nepal. These mountains are great barriers to the clouds from the south which collide into them; the resultant rainfall has created a great diversity of habitats in the Indian subcontinent.

home of Lord Siva. The ancient Hindu epic, the *Ramayana*, says of this place 'If the earth of Manasarovar touches any man's body or if he bathes in the lake, that man shall go to the paradise of Lord Brahma, or he who drinks its waters shall know the heaven of Lord Siva. Nowhere are there mountains equal to the Himalayas, for in them are both Kailash and Manasarovar.'

The scientific explanation of the birth of the Himalayas tells almost the same tale as the *Mahabharata* – and is almost as violent. Once upon a time the ancient Tethys Sea lapped the southern shores of India, which was then an island off the great southern continent of Gondwanaland. The island drifted northwards and eventually struck the coast of Asia, squeezing out the sea. As it did so, it crumpled the Earth's crust, throwing up one of the world's great mountain ranges.

The displacement of sea by land began 65 million years ago – a mere blink of an eye when you consider that the first life in the seas developed 600 million years ago and that it is 200 million years since amphibians and reptiles invaded the land. In fact, by the time the island of India crashed into Asia and created the Himalayas, some of the major groups of plants and animals were already in existence and some arrived with the crash of the island. With the creation of the Himalayas a barrier was formed, and no longer could the region facilitate the dispersal of flora and fauna. Today the Himalayas play a vital role both ecologically and because of their effect on climate – the monsoons and the climatic effect of these mountains sustain the essential food baskets of the area.

In those early times, however, on the peaks of the Himalayas, whose highest points reached almost 9 kilometres into the sky, the scarcity of food and the deathly cold winds ensured that nothing could survive for long. There is still little life above 6000 metres, but climbers have recorded tracks of mountain sheep, hares, wolves, foxes and even jumping spiders at this height. These spiders feed on tiny insects called springtails, which in turn feed on pollen, dead flies and leaf fragments blown up from the lower slopes.

The first forms of life found regularly at heights of 6000–7000 metres are lichens, of which there are said to be 16,000 species in the world. The tiny flowering plant *Stellaria decumbens*, related to the common British chickweed, grows at 6000 metres and is one of the few plants to survive at this high altitude. Algae, mosses and other plants start to appear below 6000 metres, and after these, entangled between the boulders on the snowfields, are some of the first living creatures. These creatures attract predators, and so, as you descend the mountains, the rich diversity of the Indian subcontinent, with its dazzling array of species, begins to unfold.

The extensive mountain chain that stretches across the thick neck of the Indian subcontinent for about 2500 kilometres from Afghanistan in the west to Assam in the east is roughly 160–240 kilometres wide. It straddles six countries and has three main ranges: the Hindu Kush in the west, then the Karakorams across the northern stretches of Pakistan and the territory of Jammu and Kashmir. Both these ranges have been referred to as the Trans-Himalayan Ranges and a debate still rages as to whether they are a part of the Himalayas. Finally, along the northern frontiers of India, Nepal and Bhutan, there are the Himalayas themselves, separating the subcontinent from Tibet. The Hindu Kush and the Karakorams lie beyond the reach of the monsoon and have bleaker slopes, while the Eastern Himalayas receive the full fury of the rains.

As a result, along the length of the chain is to be found an enormous diversity of climate, vegetation and wildlife. The forests range from birch at the tree line through rhododendrons, juniper, oak and conifers, to tropical broad-leafed trees at the bottom.

OVERLEAF *The great snowscapes of the Himalayas.*
This icy realm is home to some unique species of animals.

29

*Bar-headed geese migrating across the Himalayas from their breeding grounds
in Central Asia to winter in the plains of northern India.*

There are a variety of butterflies, including the yellow swallowtail, Indian tortoiseshell,
queen of Spain and blue apollo; fourteen species of reptiles and amphibians, including
toads, geckos and snakes; and many gallinaceous birds, including thirteen species of
pheasant, ten species of partridge and at least three species of quail.

Bird life of the Himalayas

The Himalayas form a gigantic wall on the eastern edges of the Kashmir valley and
extend along the western and southwestern parts. High up in the valley, at 2800–4300
metres, are numerous lakes fed by glaciers – Alpathar, Kaunsarang, Gangabal, Tulien and
Tarsar Marsar to name just a few. In the vicinity of these lakes are valleys full of flowers.
It is at these heights that trout, first imported by the British during the Raj, have
adapted to Indian streams and lakes.

The area is dotted with snow and rain-fed streams and rivers, all of which provide
fresh water to keep the bogs, marshes and other wetlands of Kashmir alive. Some of the

finest alpine lakes exist high up in the mountain folds. At the onset of autumn huge flocks of waterfowl, duck and geese fly over the Himalayan peaks and arrive in the Kashmir valley's network of lakes, marshes and ponds. Some species, notably the bar-headed goose, have been observed at remarkable heights; where many migratory birds seem to navigate their way 'round' mountains by flying through valleys, the bar-headed goose simply flies right over the top of whatever it finds in its way.

This mass migration from the Siberian snows several thousand kilometres away brings hundreds of thousands of birds wheeling into the water to feed amid great cackling and honking. Most stay until the onset of winter and frequent the wetland paradise near Srinagar, the capital of Kashmir. When the tens of thousands of mallard leave for their breeding grounds in Siberia in February and March, it is common to see 50–100 flights every evening. Many birds of prey, including the Himalayan golden eagle, are resident in the area.

The most striking of all the Himalayan birds is not a migrant but a common resident found from west to east across the chain and at heights ranging from 1200–6000 metres. The bearded vulture or lammergeyer is an enormous bird, more like an eagle than a vulture in appearance, with a feathered head and neck and a wedge-shaped tail. A tuft of bristly black feathers hangs from the chin, giving the appearance of a beard. It has a wingspan of 2.5 metres, the broadest of any bird of the region, and the adult plumage is often stained a vivid orange: it has been widely believed that this colouring comes from the iron oxide that rubs off the rocks around its nest, but this is not so.

Lammergeyers lay their eggs early in the winter and by March the young are well grown. Though mainly scavengers, they are able to hunt and kill small animals. They are famous for their habit of dropping bones from great heights in order to shatter them and thus reach the marrow within. In flight the lammergeyer specializes in rapid, contour-hugging glides and can reach speeds of 130 kilometres an hour. It is on these sweeps that it finds skeletons to shatter and bones to drop for marrow.

Perhaps surprisingly, the highest-flying bird of the Himalayas is not a vulture but the rather less exotic chough. Two species of this crow-like bird occur at these heights, a red-billed and a yellow-billed. The red-billed tends to fly even higher than the yellow-billed, but both are seen frequently at 5000 metres, have been observed at nearly 7000 metres and one sighting has been recorded by a climber on the peak of Everest – 8848 metres!

It is extraordinary how many small birds manage to overwinter in temperatures of –30°C. Along the Indus valley, dense buckthorn thickets produce orange berries which last all winter, providing a consistent food supply. In Ladakh, where the houses traditionally have flat roofs, robin accentors spend the winter in villages. The local people store fodder and firewood on their roof, providing ideal conditions for these sparrow-like birds to nest and feed.

Chir pheasants are found at 1000–3000 metres and take their name from the chir pine which they frequent. They are birds of open, grassy and scrubby slopes and sharp descents. Chirs live in family units consisting of both parents and their young. At the onset of winter these units can become flocks. These very vocal birds keep in touch through a wide variety of sounds. Their breeding season is between March and June, and they lay clutches of ten to fourteen eggs, of which only 50 per cent are believed to survive the first six months of life. The youngsters feed on insects, the adults on roots, tubers and leaves.

The western tragopan lives at altitudes of 2200–3300 metres. Of the world's forty-nine species of pheasant, it is among the most endangered. Restricted to the temperate sub-alpine zones of India and Pakistan, it thrives in dense forests of silver spruce, fir, deodar and birch, feeding mainly on fresh oak leaves, bamboo shoots, roots, seeds, acorns and berries. The male is extravagantly marked with a red-tipped crest and scarlet feathers, while the female is a duller brown. In the cold winter tragopans prefer the southern faces of the mountain systems where good shrub and bush cover is available. They have a sharp and distinctive call that distinguishes them from other species.

The cold deserts and valleys of Pakistan

Many species of plant and animal occur across the range of the Himalayas, while some have adapted specifically to the dry conditions of the west or the wet of the east. To demonstrate some of the diversity of habitats at these high altitudes, we first visit the valley of Chitral, on the northwestern frontier of Pakistan. This is one of the last strongholds of a remarkable mountain goat called the markhor. Rarely seen, even more rarely filmed, this close cousin of the ibex (which we shall meet later) is unique to the dry hills of the Western Himalayas and the Hindu Kush, and is severely endangered.

Male markhor have enormous spiral horns and long shaggy coats with beards which extend to their knees. The undercoat is not as dense as that of the ibex, so markhor winter at lower altitudes of about 2000–2500 metres. Markhor feed mainly on the foliage of the sparse holly oak forests in which they live, when necessary scrambling up into trees to eat. They may be seen balancing some 3 metres from the ground, often hanging precariously over the edges of cliffs.

To the east of Chitral lie the Plains of Deosai, usually snow-covered but for a few weeks each year a surprising oasis of flowery meadow amid this barren, frozen

*The lammergeyer, a great bearded vulture of the mountains
that dominates the high valleys of the Himalayas.*

landscape. Here there are frogs living at altitudes of over 4000 metres, and one of the largest populations of brown bears in the Himalayas.

A fully grown Himalayan brown bear can reach almost 2.5 metres in height. The colour and thickness of its coat varies, depending on the season, but it tends to be long and luxuriant during the freezing winter months. Brown bears are particularly attracted to the open meadows of the Himalayas, where they hibernate in caves and crevices among the rocky slopes. Their body size necessitates large intakes of food, especially before the long period of hibernation. Partial to honey, they also graze on roots, tubers and bulbs in the ground. They have been known to eat marmots and moles, and even occasionally domestic livestock.

Courtship and mating occur at the height of summer, and the young are born during the winter retreat. In a few months the cubs have grown enough to follow their mother in her quest for food. They remain with her till they attain maturity – anything from three and a half to five years. Brown bears have been known to live for more than forty years.

The rare Himalayan brown bear is found at high altitudes on the open peaks.

The smaller Himalayan black bear, though a forest dweller, can be found at heights of 4500 metres in the summer; here it feeds on fruit, ripe corn, walnuts, acorns, termites and meat from sheep, goats and deer. It is a voracious consumer of both fruit and meat, because it needs to build up reserves to sustain it during hibernation. There are many recorded cases of black bears chasing leopards off their kills and appropriating the carcass. They also hunt the young of the hangul or Kashmir stag. In the lower Himalayas there are often fierce fights over food, which can occur even with tigers – such an incident was witnessed by Jim Corbett, the great naturalist who worked in the foothills of the Himalayas in the early twentieth century.

Kashmir

I have been very lucky in my encounters with Himalayan black bears, and my diary notes reveal the excitement of one of them:

It is 6 a.m. and I am on my way to Dachigam National Park some 20 kilometres from Srinagar in Kashmir. It is late October and I am wrapped in a thick coat. As I approach, the area is dotted by the red and rust colours of autumn which skirt the folds of the mountains. This is the land of Himalayan black bears and hanguls and I get ready to walk around the lower reaches of the area. It is a freezing morning as we make our way through the forest.

It is a month when the Himalayan black bears are very active because of the acorns and walnuts which, as they fall to the forest floor, attract fruit-eaters. As I walk I notice a bush shaking. From it darts a vast hangul – an exquisite sight as the early morning sun dances off its back. I walk on with a tracker and suddenly he points up to the top of a tree. Lo and behold, there is a black shape eating acorns and dropping several to the forest floor, where a young Himalayan black bear feeds greedily. I squat on the ground and watch this amazing sight. A branch crackles under my foot, the young bear wheels around and the mother rushes down the tree. Standing erect on two feet, she peers at us, then with an angry snort dashes off into the forest.

A Himalayan black bear feeding on a hangul or Kashmir stag which had originally been killed by a leopard in Dachigam National Park in Kashmir.

Hangul or Kashmir stag in their last refuge, Dachigam National Park;
in the winter they move down to the lower valleys in the park.

I move on, completely stunned by this bear vision. After nearly a kilometre, during which I see some glorious mountain scenery, the tracker brings me to a halt. About 100 metres ahead four bears are feeding greedily on the forest floor. Camouflaged behind a bush, I watch, and after ten minutes slip away without disturbing them. Nearing the entrance of Dachigam, I find another bear loping across the road in front of us. They seem to criss-cross everywhere and I have had the great fortune of seeing seven Himalayan black bears in one morning.

I was also delighted to have seen the wary hangul, which is now confined to a very few areas of Kashmir. In the great valleys of Dachigam, autumn is heralded by the rutting of the hanguls, and their calls echo across the mountain slopes. During this period there is conflict between the males, but it is usually the largest male that rules the harem. After the rut, the period approaching winter is a time to rest and feed. This is when the Indian horse chestnuts, known locally as han, ripen and are devoured by the hanguls.

In fact, the deer's name derives from that of their favourite nut. The exquisite lake of Marsar nestles at 4000 metres and its icy water flows down to Dachigam, bringing with it all the nutrients necessary for creating this unique habitat for the hangul.

When I was there, Dachigam was a Himalayan paradise. It is tragic that over the last decade it should have been abused by armed insurgency, poaching and illegal felling of trees.

Several kinds of big burrowing rodents live in the mountains above Dachigam. Each colony of marmots defines its territory with dung piles and scent marks. In August the young of this stockily built creature emerge from their burrows, but many do not survive the predations of brown bears, which have been known to dig out marmot burrows.

Neighbours of the marmots are the pikas, small mouse hares which emerge from holes under rocks to forage for grasses and scrub plants. Of the twenty-five species in the world, twenty-three are found in the mountains of Central Asia. Pikas are perfectly adapted to survive extreme cold and have been found living at 5000 metres in the Himalayas, probably a record altitude for a mammal. Well insulated in their dense brown fur, the furry soles of their feet also enable them to move about on rocks. Instead of hibernating, they live through the freezing winter on grass that they collect and store near their burrows in the summer.

A family of Himalayan marmot watch intently from outside their den.

OVERLEAF *The cold, high altitude deserts of Ladakh are transformed in the summer months wherever there is a little rain or moisture.*

Into Ladakh and Tibet

The Himalayas cover 10 per cent of India's total land surface and occupy an area of 422,300 square kilometres, over 80,000 square kilometres of which are high-altitude cold deserts. Having little rainfall and sparse vegetation, these cold areas have low densities of wild animals, which need the mobility afforded by large areas to survive. This harsh ecological system, however, leads to great adaptability in both flora and fauna. The cold deserts boast 750 species of flowering plants, while the animals have thick, insulating fur, bushy tails, large nasal cavities and extra corpuscles in their blood to cope with the lack of oxygen. They can move quickly with the changing seasons.

In the highest reaches of the Western Himalayas is Ladakh, an area of rugged beauty, much like a moonscape at times. It is a mountainous land of high passes, green-bottomed valleys and vast, barren expanses. Ladakh covers 98,000 square kilometres and large parts of it are cold deserts with a rarefied atmosphere and startlingly clear night skies. Lying in the 'shadow' of the Karakorams and Himalayas, these deserts receive very little precipitation – perhaps 10 centimetres a year, in the form of snow.

In summer the landscape appears at first glance to be a dull brown but closer inspection reveals that the earth sparkles with greys, pinks, mauves and oranges, inter-spersed with brilliant green triangles where the streams flow down from the higher

The very endangered black-necked cranes are restricted to a few areas in Ladakh, Bhutan and the Tibetan plateau. They nest in these inhospitable and icy regions.

Only a small proportion of truly wild yaks survive in the Himalayas.
However, there is a large domesticated population.

ground and the meltwaters they carry are used for irrigation. What wildlife there is at these heights benefits from the reverence the Tibetan Buddhist population feels for all living things – to the west, in Islam-dominated Pakistan, many species have been hunted ruthlessly for food, whereas here they are allowed to thrive as far as the harsh conditions permit.

The lowest parts of Ladakh are the Leh, Zanskar and Nubra valleys, which lie at an average altitude of 4500 metres, while the peaks have an average height of 6000 metres. The highest mountain in Ladakh is Saser Kangri, in the Karakoram range, at 7680 metres. There are no natural forests in this 'naked' country. During the short summer, bursts of colourful wild flowers cover the mountain slopes. Seeds are generally dispersed by the wind and may have to travel long distances to ensure the survival of their species. Only 2.5 per cent of the land is under cultivation, and this is at the bottom of valleys and on the banks of rivers and torrents.

The Nubra Valley is the greenest of all, having rich and fertile soil. Its luxuriant vegetation is in sharp contrast with the barren rocky terrain elsewhere in this region. Lakes from prehistoric times dot a few of the high-altitude valleys with brackish yet stunning emerald green water. At 4000 metres they are not devoid of aquatic life and are ideal breeding grounds for migratory birds, such as bar-headed geese, brahminy ducks and black-necked cranes. Overall, some 295 bird species have been reported from Ladakh.

The black-necked crane is one of the rarest and most elusive crane species in the world, its ancient lineage dating back over 60 million years. Perhaps because of this, Buddhists accord it a particular reverence. It can be found at 3500–5500 metres and its nesting ground is among the network of marshes in the Changthang region of Eastern Ladakh. It shares this habitat with Mongolian plovers, darting yellow wagtails, short-toed larks and many redshanks.

*The bharal or blue sheep is widely distributed across the Himalayas
and is one of the most important prey for the snow leopard.*

Mountain herbivores

Ladakh boasts large populations of shaggy-coated goats and sheep, but the largest and shaggiest animal in this wilderness is the yak, which is a wild ox. It is a massive creature, weighs nearly a tonne, has horns which can measure 76 centimetres across at their widest point, and in the summer is found at an altitude of 6000 metres. The yak is an integral part of mountain life, and when domesticated provides milk, butter and a vital means of transportation.

The nayan or Tibetan wild sheep is the largest sheep species. Found in eastern Ladakh, usually above 4000 metres, its horns can measure up to 135 centimetres across. A graceful, long-legged creature, it moves over a wide range, seeking out food and water wherever it can, and is able to survive extreme cold.

One of the five subspecies of urial, the Ladakh urial or *shapu*, is considered the progenitor of the domestic sheep and is the smallest of the wild sheep. It prefers grassy slopes at altitudes of 3000–4000 metres. Adult males are distinguished by a ruff which grows from either side of the chin and down the throat. Once under threat in the western reaches of its range, because of its habit of wandering into populated areas and falling prey to indiscriminate hunters, the urial is still rare: there is thought to be a population of about a thousand in Ladakh, many of them in the Nubra valley.

Classified as something between a sheep and a goat is the bharal, which continues to baffle taxonomists. The great American naturalist George Schaller suggested that it was basically a goat but had evolved sheeplike traits as a result of living in habitats usually occupied by sheep. If this is so, then its English name of blue sheep is doubly inaccurate, as it is in fact grey with black and white striped legs. Like mountain goats, it is perfectly at home on steep cliffs, using its remarkable agility to avoid attack, but it is not confined to them as the true mountain goats, the ibex and the markhor, are. It is more frequently found on rolling grassy hills, which most people would think of as sheep country.

The bharal's rut is accompanied by clashes and displays among the males. These high-altitude battles rage on cliffs which few people can reach. After mating, the males leave to form single-sex groups which will remain together until the onset of the next snows. By moving away from the females, the males ensure that there will be enough prime pasture to feed the newborn. It is as if they were sacrificing themselves for the sake of the new generation. The young are born in summer, when food is plentiful, and the adult males return to court and mate in winter, thus beginning another cycle of life.

The Himalayan ibex survives in the highest altitudes of any mountain goat. In Russia and Mongolia it can be found as low as 500 metres, but in the Himalayas it is

The Himalayan tahr can be found across the Himalayas, at between 2500 and 4500 metres.
It is a wild goat, totally at home in precipitous terrain.

seen above the tree line, between 3000 and 5000 metres. The male ibex is 50 per cent larger than the female and has a dense, dark beard and large, thick horns that curve backwards and continue to grow throughout the animal's life. Males can be aged by counting the divisions on their horns, which are clearly defined because the horns grow very little in winter and then rapidly in spring. It is known that a male ibex can live for sixteen years. The horns of the female are much shorter and grow more slowly.

During the winter, when snow falls incessantly, ibex live on ledges, cliffs and crests where the snow is unable to accumulate, but they are vulnerable to avalanche, which kills large numbers of them each year. They feed on herbs that survive the wintry conditions and can be seen digging in the snow with their forelegs, searching for food. They owe their agility on steep rocks to a special adaptation on the inside of their hooves, which are cushioned with a soft rubber-like padding surrounded by hard edges.

The rut takes place in winter, with males adopting a stretching posture with tail raised, upper lip curled up, tongue protruding and flicking up and down. During this time the mature males boast a thick dark brown coat with a dull white 'saddle' which becomes more pronounced as they get older. Females and young males are a grey-brown colour, without the saddle.

The winter coat is shed in the spring, rubbed off on rocks and shrubs. The 'wool', which is much warmer than that of sheep, is quickly collected by local people to make into clothes. The remaining summer coat is the same light reddish-brown for both sexes.

As the summer starts, males form adult buck groups, leaving the female with their young. Pregnant ibex move away from the group for several days in order to give birth; twins are common. After a gestation period of 170–180 days, the young are born in June or July, when there is no shortage of food.

Fossil records from 10,000 to 17,000 years ago reveal that the Himalayan tahr was once found as far west as Europe. Today it is the most numerous species of mountain goat, while the Arabian and Nilgiri tahrs are seriously endangered. Adult male Himalayan tahrs stand 1 metre at the shoulder and their luxuriant mane is particularly striking; it can reach 30 centimetres in length, extending across the back and nearly touching the knees. Tahrs are often found up to 4500 metres and, unlike others of the mountain species

The unique musk deer, with its external canines, is seriously threatened as
it is hunted mercilessly for its musk – a vital ingredient in the perfume industry.

which migrate to lower ground in the winter, tend to use the same grazing grounds throughout the year. They prefer precipitous rocks, cliff faces and any dense scrub that they can find. Their diet consists of grasses and sedges in the summer, and in the winter mosses and ferns. They take in minerals by licking the surface of rocks.

One of the great Himalayan species is the musk deer, which, in the past, was evenly distributed through the southern Himalayas. However it has been harshly exploited for its musk, a vital ingredient of perfumes and indigenous medicines. In mature males the musk gland, which is located near the navel, can contain 30–45 grammes of musk.

The musk deer is not a true deer, but a primitive, deer-like ruminant. It is shy, solitary and territorial, with long, hare-like ears. It has no antlers, but the canine teeth, which are capable of moving in their sockets, are highly developed, resembling tusks, and in males can reach a length of 10 centimetres.

Musk deer inhabit areas between 2500 metres and the sub-alpine forest. Their alarm call is like a hiss; then, with a quick bound, they rush off. Their broad, splayed hooves make for excellent locomotion on soft snow, minimizing the possibility of sinking in the snow. The musk deer's coat has air-filled compartments, arranged much like a honeycomb, for enhanced insulation. It feeds on lichens, mosses, ferns and leaves. Smell plays a vital part in its life: scent marking by defecating, urination and applying secretions of the musk glands is an integral part of its behaviour and communication, while the scent of the musk is believed to influence the oestrus cycle in females.

In the upper reaches of the Himalayas, especially on the Tibetan plateau, the Tibetan antelope lives in groups of two to twelve individuals and is active at altitudes of 3000-5000 metres. Its fleece provides wool for fine *shahtoosh* shawls, so it has been hunted viciously across its range. Today it is believed that the wool is bartered for the bones of tigers on the Indo-Tibetan border.

Another great survivor of the high, open plateaux and cold deserts is the kiang or Tibetan wild ass, which is related to the wild ass of the hot deserts of Kutch (see Chapter 4). A population of 1500–2000 or so lives in small herds of about a dozen, at altitudes above 4000 metres. Two species of goat antelope occupy lower ground. The larger, known as the serow, is a reclusive inhabitant of cliffs and forested ravines; little is known of its habits. The smaller goat antelope, the ghoral, lives on grassy slopes at lower altitudes still, between 700 and 4000 metres.

To these desert species, scattered monasteries serve as oases. Urial hang around them, drinking from the monks' springs and water tanks. Buddhist tolerance makes the wildlife confiding to the point of impertinence – at the monastery of Rezong they are even known to stand on the roof.

A family of kiang or Tibetan wild ass on the dry plains of eastern Ladakh.

The grey ghost of the mountains

The benevolence of the monks cannot, however, protect these sheep and goats, oxen and asses from their natural predators. To the lover of wildlife, the Himalayas are first and foremost the land of the snow leopard. So elusive is this big cat that mountain people attribute phantom-like qualities to it, believing that it has the ability to disappear. It is certainly extremely rare, with perhaps 3000–5000 left in the world, and its numbers continue to decrease. Its pale grey coat with dark rosettes is the perfect camouflage for its rocky habitat, so that it is hard to distinguish even in comparatively open terrain and more or less invisible in snow.

Fossil evidence suggests that the snow leopard originated in China, but in the Indus valley there are rock carvings known as petroglyphs – in which the artist cuts through the dark oxidized layer of rock to the lighter layers beneath – depicting snow leopards and bharal. This suggests that both these animals have been known to the human inhabitants of the region for at least two thousand years. Today the snow leopard occurs throughout the alpine zone of the mountains of central Asia, as far north as southern

Siberia and Mongolia, and from Afghanistan and Pakistan in the west, across northern India, Nepal, Sikkim and Bhutan to the Indian state of Arunachal Pradesh in the east. It is usually found above the tree line, at altitudes of 3000 metres or more, and may reach as high as 5500 metres in summer.

The snow leopard is a little smaller than the common leopard; it may weigh up to about 45 kilogrammes, but is more normally around 30 kilogrammes. It stands about 60 centimetres tall at the shoulder, and from its nose to the tip of its luxurious tail it can measure over 2 metres. Its thick coat and large, furry paws protect it against the extreme cold. The long furry tail serves as an added layer of insulation, to be wrapped round the animal in times of need. (Among other stories attached to the snow leopard's tail, it is said in Ladakh that a mother leopard may hang hers over a rock or cliff so that her less agile cubs can climb up it.)

Solitary by nature, the adults come together only to mate. Cubs stay with their mother until they are eighteen months old, able to fend for themselves and find their own territory; they are ready to mate by the time they are two or three years of age.

Like tigers, snow leopards avoid conflict by intensive territorial marking, be it scrapes on the ground or spraying near rocks. Estimates of the size of home range vary; it has been suggested that this can be as little as 20–38 square kilometres, though some believe that a single animal may range over 100 square kilometres or more in the course of a year. In areas where prey is plentiful, ranges may overlap, but territorial marking still seems to enable individuals to avoid each other.

Like tigers, also, they are the top of the food chain and an indication of the health of the ecosystem: where the snow leopard flourishes, there must be plenty of prey species, too. The snow leopard's diet varies from pikas and hares to yaks. They are opportunistic predators able to bring down animals three times their size: if a snow leopard enters a cattle pen it can inflict heavy damage. Its most regular prey seems to be the bharal, but during the summer it also frequently kills marmots. Marmots hibernate, however, so are not available to be preyed upon in winter and it is during these months that most predation of livestock occurs. It takes a snow leopard about three to five days to eat an animal the size of a sheep, and when it is not feeding it will sit on a rocky ledge or other suitable vantage point above its kill to guard it. Snow leopards seem to enjoy resting on rock piles, ridges or cliffs where they can get a view of the area below. Although most active at dawn and dusk, they are not averse to moving during the day.

The snow leopard is the true predator of these icy climates and is intensely endangered
all across its range. It has been ruthlessly hunted for its magnificent coat.

There are many stories about the mountain people scavenging the snow leopard's kills to eat during the freezing winter. Raghunandan Singh Chundawat, a wildlife biologist who has spent a decade researching the snow leopard, described to me an encounter he observed between a local girl and the phantom of the mountains.

Before I could reach the site, one of the goats which the snow leopard had just killed had already been retrieved by a girl. The snow leopard very soon killed another animal and moved ahead. The girl immediately ran and threw it in her

The red fox of these snow-covered regions is said to pair for life.

basket with the first one. There would be enough meat for a few weeks. But the snow leopard had quickly killed a third animal some 50–60 metres away near a bush, and in her excitement the girl started pulling the third animal without noticing that the snow leopard was holding the other end of the goat. Only when it growled at her did she realize the threat and back away from the site.

I saw the villagers bring a kill home on several occasions. Amazingly there has been no record of a snow leopard attacking a human being. This is particularly extraordinary given such close encounters over food.

The snow leopard's habit of poaching livestock does, however, bring it into conflict with local pastoralists. Particularly in Nepal, where one study has reported that over a third of households in a community lost livestock to leopards, there is a risk of people taking the law into their own hands in order to protect their animals and their livelihood. Urgent action is needed in these areas if the snow leopard is to be saved.

The immense mountain ranges are also home to common leopards, just at that altitude where snow leopards cease to be found. They range from 3000 metres down to the foothills, and right across the Himalayas from west to east. As forests have been cut down, fragmentation and degradation across these mountains is commonplace, but the leopards have adapted. By living off domestic animals, they appear to have prospered to the extent that most villages in the lower and middle Himalayas now have one or more resident leopards and in some areas they are considered pests. They have, however, played a vital role in preserving the fragile ecological balance of these areas by preventing domestic animals from overpopulating them.

The leopards of these mountains are clever and elusive. The only animals they need to fear are the bears that might usurp their food. Occasional clashes between tigers and leopards also take place, but leopards usually keep their distance. They live close to rock faces and use caves, crevices and even bushes to hide in and as day shelters.

While they are often silent, their presence can be detected late in the evening by a quiet 'sawing' sound. Territorial marking by scrapes on the ground or spraying on bushes or trees are vital means of communication.

Within an adult male's range there may be two or three females. The female gives birth to two or three young and looks after them for over a year until they are able to fend for themselves. In the first few months she will hunt near her den, bringing her cubs bits of food to eat. As the cubs grow, they join in the hunting expeditions. Leopards' tree-climbing ability gives them a distinct advantage over other large predators when chasing prey, and primates such as the langur form an important part of their diet.

Other mountain predators

The snow leopard is not the only predator of these mountainous regions, nor is it the only one to attack livestock. Local people suffer even worse depredation of their flocks because of the Tibetan wolf. This is a close relation of the common wolf which occurs throughout the northern hemisphere, and is found on the open plains and in the deserts of the subcontinent. Greyish-brown in colour, the Tibetan species weighs around 20–30 kilogrammes, stands about 75–80 centimetres at the shoulder and is over a metre long. It commonly hunts in small groups: in Ladakh the largest group seen consisted of nine individuals, and two or three wolves together was more common. Like all wolves, the Tibetan species is an opportunistic feeder, and in addition to livestock, it has been known to kill ibex trapped in deep snow.

The Indian wild dog or dhole is the other canine predator of these regions. Mostly diurnal, it hunts in packs and feeds on the wild sheep and goats of Ladakh, but has been known to attack huge animals such as gaur and Indian buffalo in lowland areas. Like their African counterpart, the wild dogs have a fascinating and complex social structure, with large family groups staying together and helping to look after succeeding generations of young. Like the African wild dog, too, they have often been condemned as brutal because of their highly efficient hunting techniques, and were until recently treated as vermin in parts of India.

The highlands of Ladakh and the edges of Tibet are also home to the Himalayan lynx. Larger than the caracal, the lynx is distinguished by long, erect tufts of hair on the tips of its ears. It is a little smaller than the snow leopard, standing about 50 centimetres at the shoulder, but is much slighter in build and has a very short tail. Active in the dense vegetation at 2500–3500 metres, it is an excellent climber and preys on hares, birds, rodents and occasionally young goats and sheep. If it is unable to eat all its kill at one sitting, it will hide or even bury the remains to avoid losing them to scavengers.

More recently the tiger has entered the land of the snow leopard. There have often been reports of tigers in Bhutan at 2400–4000 metres, and on the western flank of the Himalayas above and near Corbett National Park in Uttar Pradesh tigers are occasionally seen at 1500 metres. But never before have there been reports of tigers in southeastern Tibet, where the Yarlung Tsangpo River becomes the Brahmaputra before sweeping down the eastern Himalayas. Observers have tracked the Bengal tiger crossing the

The Royal Bengal tiger has recently been recorded negotiating high passes through the snow on to the Tibetan plateau at nearly 4500 metres.

Chimdro La Pass at 4570 metres into the northern slopes of the Himalayas where tigers have never been reported before. In less than two years the tigers of this high-altitude region have killed over 300 domestic animals. It appears that they have been pushed up the slopes as lowland forested tracts are lost to agriculture and as human disturbances increase. Even in Bhutan they have been recorded at over 4000 metres. These snow-splattered Himalayan tigers are probably coming into contact with the snow leopard for the first time ever.

East into Nepal

While I was in Nepal I had the extraordinary experience of discovering Namobuddha, a site where Buddha is said to have given up his life to feed a starving tigress and her cubs. It was an extraordinary thing to discover at 2000 metres above sea level! For me it was like a final pilgrimage, because nearly sixteen years ago I had read of such a place but never knew that it really existed. This monastery or *gompa* had tigers in bronze painted on the doors, and right on the peak of a hill up which I clambered was a stone frieze where Buddha's sacrifice is depicted.

The sun was setting, lighting up the black stone – over fifty candles created an eerie light and I stood rooted to the spot. I will never forget that moment: as the wind raced across the mountains, I knew that I was in the tiger's temple. Below me Buddhist monks chanted, prayer wheels rolled and I thought of the Himalayas and how, at Namobuddha, the tiger had been imprinted on them forever.

Some of the gorges in these mountains are spectacular. In central Nepal, in the heart of the Himalayas, is the valley of Kali Gandaki, said to be the deepest gorge in the world. It separates two of the greatest mountains on Earth, Dhaulagiri and Annapurna, each of which has a peak in the snow line at 7850 metres. The widest part of the gorge between these mountains is 22 kilometres, and at its central point the bed of the river that flows between them is 5600 metres below. Ammonites found in this area reveal that these mountains were raised from what must have been part of the sea bed. Occasionally, boulders can be seen streaked with orange, which is calcium carbonate from the remains of sea animals.

The gorge at Kali Gandaki illustrates the diversity that can occur in one valley system. The upper part is dry because the monsoon dies out on the southern slopes and little rain penetrates the valley floor. This semi-desert area is spotted with hardy shrubs, yet is only a few kilometres from lush vegetation.

A typical rhododendron forest in the mountains of central Nepal.

In the tropical areas of Kali Gandaki dramatic waterfalls punctuate the thick pine forests that hug the valley slopes and extend down to the river. Himalayan griffon vultures soar in the skies above. Lower down, groves of rhododendron, their branches patchworked with lichens, reveal the changing terrain. The scale and grandeur of gorges like this provoke wonder and awe. In fact, the spiritual effects on local inhabitants, both Hindu and Buddhist, led them to build temples at Muktinath on the western flank of Annapurna. These temples are places of pilgrimage and give solace to travellers of all kinds. Migratory birds passing between the plains of India and the highlands of central Asia quench their thirst at the temple water tanks.

Valleys of flowers: the eastern Himalayas

Further east, where the lower Himalayas meet the plains, lush forests cover the ranges and here the mountains intercept the moisture-laden winds from the ocean. These eastern forests get the full brunt of the monsoon and have their own very special species. In the west, there is obvious influence from Africa, the Mediterranean or Europe.

When the snow-covered plateaux awake after eight months of winter, they briefly become flowery meadows which envelop the senses. In Sikkim, nestling between Nepal and Bhutan, and in Arunachal Pradesh, the easternmost state of India, the flowers create vivid splashes of colour with pink rhododendrons and orchids that sparkle in the

The exquisite blue poppy (left) and saussurea (above), typical flowers of many high altitude valleys in the mountains. Plants and flowers have created mechanisms to protect themselves from heavy rain and cold.

OPPOSITE *A tree orchid from the* Vanda *family found in the foothills of the eastern Himalayas bordering India and Bhutan.*

*The satyr tragopan, now confined to the wooded mountains
of central and eastern Himalayas.*

thick forest. At 4000–5000 metres lies the land of blue poppies. These flowers adorn the
meadows and their armoury of straw-coloured spines protrudes from leafy rosettes,
stems and sepals.

In the alpine zone of the eastern Himalayas flowering plants have two fundamental
problems: the cold and the raging monsoon. They have adapted in various ways. A
plant called the saussurea wraps itself in a gauze of fibres to protect it from heavy rain
and to provide insulation against the cold. A micro-climate inside enables the seed to
grow and the flowers to form – like a high-altitude greenhouse. The saussurea's root
has strong medicinal properties and it is used to cure fevers, coughs, asthma and even
cholera. The Himalayan edelweiss grows a bunch of protective leaves that surround the
flower. The gentian's vase-shaped flowers dwarf the mother plant in an effort to attract
insects, but the first drops of rain will close them to prevent drowning. On the moist
lowland slopes, some flowers extend long aerial roots that sink into the moss of tree
trunks and soar to 30 metres or more. This lofty perch ensures efficient propagation by

birds, which eat the fruit and excrete the seeds below. The Himalayan balsam nestles in shady gullies, being tolerant of both wet and shade. When the fruit ripens the pod explodes, shooting the seeds 2.5 metres across the forest floor to aid propagation.

The eastern Himalayas are also the true home of orchids, which are the most highly evolved and complex of flowers, blooming in an array of vivid and startling colours. There are supposed to be at least 24,000 species of orchids in the world, and new ones are frequently being discovered. They are found across the world from tropical forests to alpine meadows and even into the snow line. The word is derived from the Greek orchis, which means 'testis'; the plant is so named because of the sexually healing properties of its flowers and roots.

It is estimated that there are 800 species of orchids in India, and in the Eastern Himalayas from Sikkim and Darjeeling to Mizoram there are at least 455. Species such as *Galeola falconeri*, *Chilochista lunifera*, *Renanthera imschootiana*, *Eulophia nuda*, *Arachnanthe cathcartii*, *Vanda coerulea*, *Dendrobium devonianum* and many more flourish here.

The bird life of the eastern Himalayas is also very different from that of the west. At least nineteen species have been classified as endemic. The exquisite Ward's trogon is found only in the broad-leafed evergreen forest of the region, while the rufous-necked hornbill occurs in Thailand and Myanmar, but on the subcontinent is confined to Arunachal Pradesh.

Of the many species of pheasant found here, the male satyr tragopan or horned pheasant is the most colourful. At the peak of his splendid courtship display he unfurls an electric blue wattle on his throat and erects a pair of fleshy horns on his head.

Blood pheasants forage for pine shoots, mosses, ferns and lichen in what must be the world's highest pheasant habitat – the melting snows at 2700–4500 metres. The 'blood' in their name comes from the male's crimson markings, whose brilliance is matched by few other birds. The females are dull in colour, but this provides them with excellent camouflage when they are incubating their eggs in grass-lined gaps between boulders.

Some remarkable descriptions of pheasants in the east come from William Beebe. In his book *Pheasant Jungles*, published in 1927, he wrote:

At Pungatong I added silver pheasants and peacock pheasants to my note books and collection of skins. In the jungle here brilliant wine and chestnut-coloured trogons swung from branch to branch, great hornbills flew overhead with a roar of wings like a rushing wind, pearl-gray monkeys watched me with never-quenched curiosity. One of my most unexpected finds came when I was stalking jungle-fowl. In the bed of a half-dried stream I saw unexpectedly a wallowing, mud-caked back and heard loud snorting. Mechanically I jumped for the nearest tree, and was just swinging myself up out of reach when the creature raised its head and instead of the low swung horns of a water buffalo I saw, to my astonishment, a long, upright unicorn – it was a huge rhinoceros, rare indeed at this latitude, and elevation of over half a mile.

Beebe also wrote this striking description of the monal pheasant or *impeyan*:

When the shadow of a cloud slips along the mountain slope the impeyan glows dully – its gold is tempered, its copper cooled, its emerald hues veneered to a pastel of iridescence. But when the clear sun again shines, the white light is shattered on the impeyan's plumage into a prismatic burst of color.

My eye caught a trembling among the maiden-hair fern, and I swung my glass and brought a full-plumaged impeyan into the field. The dew and soft light of early dawn deadened his wonderful coat. His clear brown eyes flashed here and there as he plucked the heads of tiny flowers from among the grass.

For fifteen minutes nothing more happened; then for the space of an hour impeyans began to appear singly or in pairs, and once three together. Finally fourteen birds, all cocks in full plumage, were assembled. They gathered in a large glade which already showed signs of former work, and there dug industriously, searching for grubs and succulent tubers. They never scratched like common fowl, but always picked, picked with their strong beaks. Every three or four seconds they stood erect, glanced quickly about, and then carefully scanned the whole sky. It was easy to divine the source of their chief fear – the great black eagles which float miles high like motes. The glittering assemblage fed silently, now and then uttering a subdued guttural chuckle.

When the sun's rays reached the glade, the scene was unforgettable: fourteen moving, shifting mirrors of blue, emerald, violet, purple, and now and then a flash of white, set in the background of green turf and black, newly upturned loam.

The most appealing mammal resident of the eastern Himalayas is the red panda. It is solitary and secretive, arboreal and nocturnal, and therefore rarely seen. It looks rather like a teddy bear, with a round head, upright ears and short muzzle, and is a lovely reddish-orange to rich brown colour. Its bushy tail is marked with thick white rings. Its face is white with red stripes, and the underside of its body, including its legs,

*Endemic to the eastern Himalayas, the red panda is an elusive creature
that lives in the temperate forests above 1500 metres.*

is black. The soles of its feet are matted and hairy, like those of polar bears, and its
well-developed toes and semi-retractable claws make it adept at climbing trees.

Red pandas live in bamboo thickets above 2000 metres and feed on bamboo
sprouts, grasses, leaves, fruits and sometimes even eggs, grubs and insects, which add
protein to their diet. With a call like that of a child, they occupy small home ranges,
marked by a series of scent posts and preferred resting spots. They are able to leave a
scent trail by ejecting a strong odour from their anal gland, which enables one panda to
find another – especially important, of course, during courtship and mating. Red pandas
are habitual scent-markers, straddling wooden stumps or any protruding object and
depositing scent from their anal glands. Males can also squirt their urine. It is said that
even the pores on the palms of the red panda's 'hands' leave a scent on the forest floor.

Females reproduce once a year, giving birth to one or two young after a gestation period of just over four months. Both giant and red panda babies are the same weight at birth, though the giant panda is four times larger when fully grown. Young red pandas are usually hidden in large tree holes or cavernous openings, seeing nothing of the outside world for their first three months. During this time they are cared for by both parents. The young are generally independent by the age of nine months.

The golden langur

We end this phase of our journey at what must be one of the most magnificent spots in the entire Indian subcontinent: the lower eastern Himalayas near the Manas River. It was at the edge of this river that I was fortunate to come across a troop of golden langurs, the world's rarest monkey. This beautiful and timid creature has an exceptionally long tail with a tassel at the end, a generous golden ruff around its otherwise hairless black face and an exquisite coat which changes colour through the seasons, ranging from golden brown through cream to white, and glowing truly golden in bright sunlight.

First reports of langurs in cream-coloured coats were made by an officer of the Bengal Forest Department as recently as 1907, and the next recorded sighting was at the Manas Wildlife Sanctuary in Assam in 1947. They are now confined to a small patch of the forest on the Manas River, which forms the border between the Manas Wildlife Sanctuary in Bhutan and the Manas National Park in India. Large portions of their habitat are in Bhutan, where they were once numerous in the forests of the Black Mountain Range. The population in 1960 was thought to be about 550. However, 180 were counted in Assam in 1978, and 1200 in Bhutan in 1980.

The golden langur thrives in dense tropical forests, particularly among deciduous trees. Non-aggressive, diurnal and exclusively vegetarian, it spends most of its time in trees, descending to the ground only for water. Like all langurs, it is capable of prodigious leaps from branch to branch. Troops can comprise as many as forty animals controlled by a dominant male.

As I drove through the forest of Manas on the Indian side, watching for langurs in the tree canopy, the mountains of Bhutan suddenly loomed over the grasslands like a mirage. At sunset the river sparkled, winding its way around the edge of the Himalayas. My first sight of it took my breath away. Great pied hornbills swept above me, filling the air with their raucous call. I sat on the riverbank and watched the light fade as the black shapes of the mountains reached for the darkening sky. At about eight in the evening the wind started whistling across the hills, and soon a half-moon peeped out to

The golden langur of the eastern foothills of the Himalayas is restricted to small pockets in Assam and along the Manas River in Bhutan. These are its only homes on the planet.

be reflected in the water. Manas is a place of peace, serenity and unmatched beauty. Within these foothills elephants, tigers, rhinos, wild buffaloes, gaur, hog deer, swamp deer and so much more touch the splendour of the Himalayas.

From here the Manas River flows south, eventually joining the great Brahmaputra, which will carry its water on to the flood-plains of Bangladesh. Our journey now takes us to those flood-plains, where some of the subcontinent's richest wildlife abounds.

OVERLEAF *A group of wild buffalo on the banks of the Manas River, below the foothills of the Bhutan Himalayas.*

CHAPTER TWO

SACRED
WATERS

MY CHILDHOOD MEMORY of the Gangotri glacier, the source of the Ganges, is still strong. At the age of ten, I had managed to trek to an altitude of nearly 4000 metres, to a place where, amid the chants of thousands of pilgrims, a gurgling stream gives birth to India's most sacred river. The Ganges emerges from an ice cave – known as Gomukh, 'the cow's mouth' – at the foot of Gangotri, surrounded by some of the mightiest peaks of the Himalayas.

Hindu mythology tells us that in this icy setting, in order to save the Earth from the rushing waters of the heavenly river Ganga, the god Siva caught the river on his brow and checked its course through his matted locks. The waters then descended from Siva's brow in a series of different streams, one of which was the Ganges.

Known at its source as the Bhagirathi, the river becomes the Ganges only when it unites with the Alaknanda at Devprayag, some 300 kilometres downstream. After a further 2500 kilometres it joins up with the mighty Brahmaputra, which has already flowed almost 3000 kilometres from its own source across the Himalayas in southern Tibet. The two rivers wind their way through villages, towns, cities and fragments of wilderness till they unite to form the River Padma and empty into the Bay of Bengal by way of the largest delta in the world. When the rains come the rivers burst their banks and the waters spread over vast areas of land. The volume of water at this season is awesome – even stream beds that are dry the rest of the year gurgle with life and at the height of the monsoon the rivers discharge 800 million gallons of water into the Bay of Bengal every second. In the course of its journey the Ganges turns from a sparkling mountain stream into a huge, sluggish and muddy river, and along the way it creates some phenomenal wildlife habitats.

But how does the life-giving monsoon come about? Its name derives from the Arabic word for the seasonal winds of the Arabian Sea that blow for six months from the

Gomukh, the source of the Ganges, at nearly 4000 metres: a sadhu gets ready for his icy dip below the glacier. This place is sacred to millions of pilgrims.

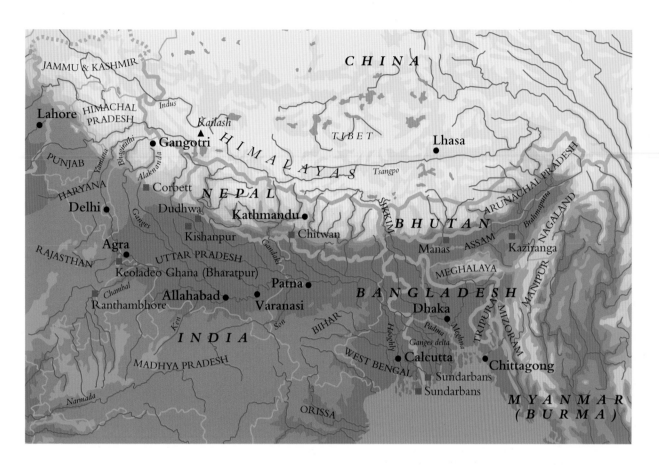

northeast, then six months from the southwest. In India, however, the word 'monsoon' is generally applied to the rain that falls between June and September.

Much of the Asian climate results from the seasonal movements of air masses. Central and southern Asia, for example, have cooler winters but much hotter summers than Pacific and Atlantic areas on the same latitudes. The root of this variation in temperature is the Indian monsoon, which manifests itself differently in different areas.

The northeast monsoon arises from dry continental winds, resulting in clear or lightly clouded skies and occasional light rain. This dry monsoon lasts from the middle of December to the end of May. The southwest monsoon, on the other hand, arises from ocean winds, which bring high humidity and frequent, heavy rain. This wet

LEFT *The Ganges, just below the mountain town of Devprayag. For its entire journey of 2500 kilometres the river is the very lifeblood for millions of people and for a rich diversity of wildlife.*

OVERLEAF *The Corbett National Park in the foothills of the western Himalayas. The Ramganga River flows through the Sivalik hills creating some of the finest wilderness of the region.*

monsoon runs from June to September. As it retreats southwards to the equatorial belt between September and December, the rainfall gradually diminishes.

In May, India commonly experiences extremely high temperatures because the highlands and mountains of the north prevent any cold air from reaching the plains. By June the thermometer hits 45°C and everyone starts scanning the sky for signs of the relief-bringing monsoon. When the moisture-laden winds eventually sweep across from Arabia, they hit the steep Western Ghats and then the dry heat of the inland air. This 'collision' forces the clouds to drop their precious burden, and the windward slopes of the Western Ghats receive 200–500 centimetres of rain in a series of violent thunderstorms. Over the Ganges valley the air currents are deflected by the Himalayas and pushed upwards, while a southeasterly air flow forces the water vapour to condense in torrents.

Monsoon winds sweep westward from Myanmar across the Bay of Bengal and then hit northeastern parts of the subcontinent, such as Chittagong in Bangladesh and Puri in the state of Orissa. When the winds reach the hills of Assam, they are boxed in by the eastern Himalayas. Forced suddenly upwards, the clouds burst and the area below receives some of the heaviest rain in the world.

Similar clashes between winds, clouds and mountains happen all over the subcontinent. Where they occur in conjunction with very high temperatures, they create some of the wettest forests known to man, as we shall see in Chapter 5.

The Gangetic Plain

Below the foothills of the Himalayas exist some of the subcontinent's most fertile forests. Here, too, is the Gangetic Plain, the richest wildlife area in India. Because the Ganges is partially snow-fed, it is a reliable, year-round source of water in a country where many rivers are parched in the summer. The most productive terrain of all is the *terai*, a flat, marshy strip of land 50–60 kilometres wide that stretches 1600 kilometres across the foothills and the Gangetic Plain, extending across northern India to touch Nepal, Bhutan and Bangladesh. The soil here is wet clay: the rainfall varies from 100 centimetres in the west to 200 centimetres in the east. This richly productive area has given rise to wonderful riverine tracts of forest where both the tiger and the elephant live – areas of breathtaking natural beauty rarely seen elsewhere. However, under enormous

Monsoon clouds gather over the bird paradise at Bharatpur – another season is about to start.

pressure from agriculture and development, the area has become fragmented, with disastrous consequences for the wildlife.

In the west, for example, the fate of the local populations of Indian rhino has been sealed forever because their grassland habitat has been given over almost completely to sugar-cane cultivation. Huge efforts to reintroduce the rhino have been made in Dudhwa, on the borders of India and Nepal, and some females have produced calves. But years after this project was started the rhinos still remain enclosed in an area of 25 square kilometres and it is unlikely that they will ever be freed. Dudhwa must once have had wonderful stretches of *terai* grassland where both tiger and swamp deer flourished, but now only fragments remain. Indeed, all the lush forests bordering Dudhwa in Nepal have been converted into farmland, so this stretch of the India/Nepal border does not have a single tree on the Nepal side.

However, some national parks in the area still display the great diversity of the region. Fragments of grassland, with elephant grass and tracts of dense forest, manage to survive, and the giant herbivores of India still exist. Nearly 20,000 elephants roam India and a large proportion of them inhabit the Gangetic Plain. Among the many rivers, lakes and swamps of the *terai* the gharial or long-snouted crocodile and the mugger or marsh crocodile make their homes. Here, too, is India's greatest bird sanctuary, the Keoladeo Ghana National Park – better known by its old name of Bharatpur. Formerly the shooting preserve of the Maharaja of Bharatpur, where in 1938 the Viceroy of India's party shot 4273 birds in one day, the park, near Agra in Rajasthan, is now a haven where 300 species of bird may be seen within an area of 29 square kilometres.

But the Ganges is more than a source of water and life. The beliefs of millions of Hindus across India are entangled with this river. They believe it will cleanse their soul, forgive them their sins and carry away the ashes of their dead. On the banks of the Ganges stands the holy city of Varanasi (formerly Benares), where thousands of steps (known as *ghats*) lead down to the river and enable the faithful to bathe in the sacred waters. To the Hindus Varanasi is the centre of the world. Here, every March, hundreds of thousands of people flock to celebrate the festival of Mahasivaratri, one of the many festivals to Siva. India's normally rigid caste system is temporarily thrown aside as men and women from all walks of life – some of whom have saved for years to make this once-in-a-lifetime journey – bathe side by side, united in their faith in the cleansing power of Mother Ganga.

Almost unnoticed in the middle of this religious fervour the cycle of life continues. At this time of year the rivers have contracted into their beds; for the first time in months there is a clear distinction between land and water. As the temperature rises the sandbanks grow hotter and the eggs of the soft-shelled freshwater turtles hatch. For these turtles it is a time of plenty: they are opportunistic and almost indiscriminate feeders adapted to murky waters, and they gorge themselves on the detritus of the seething human activity.

At the age of nine I immersed the ashes of my grandfather in the waters near the city of Hardwar. But my feeling for this river concerns its ability to sustain a very special wildlife habitat, and not its religious inspiration.

Life on the alluvial plains

Let us begin our journey in late summer, when the monsoon waters spill on to the flood-plain and for 1500 kilometres along the margins of the Himalayas countless tributaries of the Ganges and the Brahmaputra are bursting from the hills like muddy champagne. Crops are destroyed, wildlife and people are drowned and areas of high ground become isolated sanctuaries. But the monsoons are great providers to both man and animal, and cannot be seen as purely destructive. The rivers carry huge quantities of silt from the uplands – which accounts for the muddy colour of the floodwaters – and these deposits of silt are what make the plains so fertile, and able to support such a wealth of wildlife. This fertility is also responsible for making the region a productive food basket for millions of people.

At the onset of the monsoon the shrieking call of the koel or Indian cuckoo can be heard as it flashes across the sky chasing other birds, especially crows, away from their nests. While the chasing goes on, the female koel darts into the vacated nest and quickly lays her eggs. The nest owner returns to find some extra eggs in her nest, but guards them nonetheless. The koels leave, satisfied that their young will emerge and be looked after by their adoptive parent. Come the next monsoon, this remarkable trick will be played again before the black clouds gather and fill the skies. It seems extraordinary that the crows do not notice anything amiss: up to 13 koel's eggs have been found in a single crow's nest, whose normal complement of eggs is no more than four or five.

Two rare birds, the swamp francolin and the endangered Bengal florican are endemic to the *terai* and *duars* of Assam and are restricted to protected areas. The clay soil and high rainfall provide the vegetation necessary for their survival.

Little is known of the habits of either of these birds. The great ornithologist Salim Ali describes the swamp francolin or swamp partridge as a 'confirmed skulker, taking to wing reluctantly'. Its brown and buff colouring blend with its surroundings, and it nests among weeds and grass, so it is particularly difficult to spot.

The Bengal florican is easier to observe because of its extravagant mating display. One of the rarest members of the bustard family, its estimated population is fewer than 500. It is about the size of a small goose, the female slightly larger and taller than the male, and both sexes have black heads and buff-brown backs. Breeding males have wings of pure white feathers. Normally a timid bird, it conceals itself by 'squatting' in high grass, but during courtship the male attracts the female by displaying and fluffing up his feathers. Displays can last for many hours as the males jump, fly and glide around the female in great, energetic bursts of activity.

Bharatpur, a bird paradise

This is a time of plenty for the birdlife of the Gangetic Plain. The fish on which many of them feed synchronize their breeding so that their young can grow very quickly – but because the rivers have burst their banks, a glut of all sorts of aquatic food for the birds is spread over what would normally be dry land.

Since the start of the monsoon, visiting birds have been gathering from all over northern India, converging on Bharatpur to breed. The first to arrive are the herons, followed by egrets, cormorants, ibis, spoonbills and storks, then the winter migrants from the Arctic tundra and western Siberia – numerous species of ducks, geese, coots, eagles, harriers, cranes and waders. The new arrivals merge with the residents and a cacophony of noise results as they get down to feeding on the millions of fingerling fish in the water.

Cormorants, darters, spoonbills, ibises, herons, egrets, cranes, pelicans, flamingoes, geese, ducks, larks, chats, kites, buntings, eagles, harriers, owls, vultures, kingfishers and many more are a part of this vibrant wetland, building nests in an estimated 50,000 trees.

When I first went to Bharatpur as a boy I was stunned at the sound and sight of hundreds of species of birds. Wherever you look, fascinating sights meet the eye: painted storks break off nesting materials, completely engrossed in the building of their home; fishing eagles swoop to catch their prey; pintail ducks dive for their prey, waggling their bottoms in the air. On all sides Bharatpur is alive with squawking, eating, nesting, mating and grooming.

Seven of the world's seventeen species of stork are found here, the most numerous and eye-catching being the painted stork, a large, long-legged, long-necked bird, rather ungainly on land but with an elegant soaring flight. It is predominantly white with black and white wings, earning the description 'painted' from the oddly contrasting pink patches on its back, orangey-pink head and legs and a paler yellowy-pink bill.

A painted stork gathers material for its nest on the flood-plains of northern India.

The painted stork's breeding success seems to depend largely on the strength of the monsoon: the greater the rainfall, the more fish there are for the storks to feed on, and the more young they manage to rear. A colony returns year after year to the same trees, where the males choose a nesting site and defend a territory. Courtship takes the form of an elaborate bowing ritual and is followed by a period of concentrated nest-building. When this is completed a single tree may be full of nests as little as 30 centimetres apart.

Each female lays between two and four eggs and for the month's incubation period she and her mate take turns to guard the nest. Once the young hatch they grow rapidly and have to be fed ever increasing quantities of fish. A census carried out in the 1940s by the great ornithologist Dr Salim Ali reached the conclusion that the painted storks alone consumed some 60 tonnes of fish in the course of a breeding season!

Fortunately the storks are very efficient anglers, wading in shallow water to stir up the mud and fish at their feet. They feed their young not with live fish but by regurgitating partly digested food for them. The young therefore have to compete and the smaller chicks frequently lose out to stronger siblings: an average of one per nest survives to adulthood.

Rather smaller and drabber than the painted stork but similar in habits and often found nesting nearby is the open-billed stork. It owes its name to the strange arch in its mandibles which makes it look as if its mouth is hanging open. No one really understands the purpose of the open bill: one suggestion is that it may act as a 'shell opener', helping the bird to extract freshwater snails from their shells, but as this activity takes place largely underwater, it has not been observed frequently enough to confirm the theory.

Open-billed storks are revered as a sign of prosperity in some parts of India, because they arrive at a time of maximum growth, when crops are at their peak. At Joginagar village, near Shantiniketan, in Bengal the people carefully guard a colony of birds that has chosen to take up residence there for five or six months each year during the monsoon;

LEFT *A pair of Sarus cranes, endemic to the subcontinent.*
They are a great symbol in folklore of fidelity and harmony.

OVERLEAF *Siberian cranes visit Bharatpur's wetlands each year from*
their breeding grounds thousands of kilometres away to the north in Russia.
This highly endangered species has declined, and only four birds visited
Bharatpur in the winter of 1996–7.

an old man in the village even reared and hand-fed two nestlings that had fallen out of a tree. At its peak the stork population is about 8000, nearly three times the population of the village. The storks' droppings are considered some of the best natural fertilizers for agricultural fields, and nesting colonies are carefully protected.

Four species of crane visit Bharatpur, but the Sarus crane is resident. A large grey bird with a red head and nearly as tall as a man, it is much venerated as a symbol of marital bliss in India. Sarus cranes pair for life and locals believe that if one dies, the other will die of a broken heart. The Sarus's courtship displays is one of the most magnificent bird spectacles in the world. The couple bow, circle round each other with outspread wings, throw back their long necks, take great leaps into the air – and all the while uttering their far-reaching, trumpeting call. Sometimes the display culminates in mating, but often it seems to be an end in itself and the birds go back to whatever they were doing.

The snow-white Siberian crane is a regular winter visitor to Bharatpur, but is now seriously endangered. Its total population across the world is less than 2000 and its decline is indicated in the numbers that visit Bharatpur – four in 1996 as opposed to 200 in 1965. A huge effort to protect it is now underway, but its status is critical.

Bharatpur is the permanent home of four species of eagles: the Pallas fishing eagle, the short-toed eagle, the tawny eagle and the lesser spotted eagle. It is also the winter home of five other eagle species, including the crested serpent eagle, a local migrant that comes to feast on the countless snakes that breed in the wetland. Other winter visitors include the Bonelli's hawk eagle, the imperial eagle, the greater spotted eagle and the steppe eagle. Even the white-tailed sea eagle has occasionally visited Bharatpur. There is ample prey for them all; indeed, the Pallas fishing eagle, which has been known to catch 6-kilogramme fish, is also partial to geese, ducks and the young of nesting birds, such as ibises and storks. Marsh and pale harriers live off coots, moorhens and even pond herons. The pale harrier has been known to migrate distances of 8000 kilometres, flying individually rather than in flocks, but with a group sometimes congregating at particular spots each evening.

Dusk in the wetlands is owl time. The most spectacular of Bharatpur's eight species is the Indian eagle owl or great horned owl, but dusky horned owls, mottled wood owls, spotted owlets and collared scops owls are found in the woodlands near the water's edge.

Many years ago I made a memorable trip, drifting silently in a little boat on the waters of Bharatpur, completely engrossed with the variety of sound, colour and activity. Eagles, ready to pounce on their prey, glided above me, turtles basked on logs of wood,

The crested serpent eagle is a ferocious predator of snakes and lizards; it is found
in forested tracts across peninsular India and up to 3000 metres in the Himalayas.

the snake-like neck of the darter appeared and disappeared, while the hovering pied
kingfisher pierced the water with its sharp eyes in search of fish. Each little niche in this
wetland has its own pattern of life, and all these niches form part of the intricate
mosaic that is Bharatpur.

River life

Birds are, of course, not the only creatures that migrate. One of the great fish of Indian river basins is the mahseer, which is widely distributed from east to west. Six species of this large, scaly freshwater fish inhabit the subcontinent. The largest is the golden mahseer, which can reach the phenomenal length of 2.7 metres and is found in sub-Himalayan rivers. Known as the Himalayan salmon, it is considered the subcontinent's finest game fish. It spends most of its life in the lowlands, but migrates upstream each year, breeding at a point above that where the Alaknanda and the Bhagirathi join to form the Ganges. Other species of mahseer are found in water temperatures ranging from 6°C to 35°C and at heights ranging from sea level to 2000 metres.

The mahseer devours small fish with relish, but is actually omnivorous and also eats weeds, grasses, bamboo seeds, snails, aquatic insects, larvae and crabs. Unlike other carnivorous fish, it has no teeth to hold its prey, but it has thick lips for sucking soft material. The mahseer's feeding habits make it an effective agent for weed control, so it holds an important place in the river systems of India. It is also a vital foodstuff for many different predators, including fishing eagles, otters and crocodiles.

Many of the 33 species of tortoise and turtle recorded on the subcontinent are endemic and live along the Brahmaputra, the Ganges, the Indus and their flood-plains. Their body armour, evolved from reptilian scales, is reinforced by bone underneath and is essential for survival. The body within the shell is rigid, with the ribs fused to the bony plates, while the parts outside the shell – the head, neck, limbs and tail – move freely. Freshwater species have the ability to retract these parts into the shell. Turtles are omnivorous scavengers feeding opportunistically – like those at Varanasi – on whatever is available.

These feeding habits are of great benefit to the environment. Turtles clean out seas, rivers and lakes, clearing water weeds that would otherwise choke up channels and create stagnant pools which are great breeding grounds for mosquitoes and malaria. Some turtles eat snails, helping to control diseases that these tiny creatures can transmit. Others scavenge on dead animals and plants, even dead human beings committed to the holy waters of the Ganges. Not only does this clear unwholesome debris from the rivers, but when the digested food passes through their system, vital nutrients are released into the water.

Turtles feature strongly in Hindu mythology, but one of the rarest species owes its survival to its connection with a Muslim saint. The black soft-shelled turtle is today found in only one place – a tank measuring 100 x 61 metres, which is attached to an Islamic shrine near Chittagong in Bangladesh. It is protected by the custodians of the shrine and nearly 300 of the species may be found there. How they arrived in the tank is unknown. Locals believe that the turtles were human sinners whom the thirteenth-century saint transformed into reptiles as punishment for their evil deeds. It is also believed that eating mud off the back of these turtles helps barren women to conceive. About a dozen stalls within the shrine compound sell cattle offal, prawns, fish, bread, puffed rice, tea leaves and bananas, which pilgrims can skewer on to thin bamboo or wooden sticks and present to the turtles as an offering.

Although these turtles are carefully looked after, the species remains desperately vulnerable. Because each individual is considered sacred, it is forbidden to remove any of them to attempt to set up a breeding colony elsewhere. If disease or some other disaster struck, the black soft-shelled turtle could be lost for ever.

Great rivers are the focus of many sacred beliefs, and the Gangetic freshwater dolphin is another creature that features in Hindu myth. Just as Siva created the life-giving River Ganges from his flowing hair, so he gave birth to the dolphin or bhagirath to spread the news that the river was coming. This sacred messenger nowadays brings more pertinent information about the river basins, its presence being a sign of healthy water. Rare and elusive, its population in India, Bangladesh and Nepal totals about 4000-5000, but the Ganges and its tributaries may be home to no more than 500-700.

The dolphin has had to learn to survive in the murky waters of the Ganges, where its vision is completely useless. As a result its eyes are mere vestiges of what they must once have been, lacking even a lens with which to focus. The Gangetic dolphin 'sees' entirely through sound, producing – like its better known marine relative – a constant flow of ultrasonic clicks whose echoes enable it to create a picture of its surroundings, including potential prey.

A local migrant, the Gangetic dolphin may sometimes be found sharing a patch of water with a few others, although it is not gregarious. It is a slim, swift animal with an elongated snout forming the beak, which is separated from the forehead by a prominent groove. Its jaw is well adapted for browsing on the river bed, where it feeds on cuttle-fish and crustaceans. It catches fish with a sideways snap of its jaws – a characteristic it shares with the largest and most spectacular of the Indian reptiles, the gharial. Thanks to a combination of hunting and habitat loss, the gharial, a species of Indian crocodile, almost died out in the 1970s, but recent conservation efforts including very successful captive breeding schemes mean that thousands have now been released back into the wild.

Crocodiles are the closest living relatives of the dinosaurs, and the fact that they have survived so long with very little change to their physical characteristics is a tribute to their evolutionary design. Some of their unusual features include a four-chambered heart, socketed teeth, a plate which separates the mouth from the nasal channels, and spongy lungs. Their protective covering of bony dorsal plates is not joined to the underlying skeleton, a feature which enables them to move at surprising speeds.

The gharial is distinguished by the strange swollen growth (known as a *ghara*, which in Hindi means 'earthen pot') on the tip of the male's snout. The *ghara* is useful during courtship, when males compete for the favour of females and their rivalry is expressed in loud hisses that resonate in their snouts and carry across the water. The *ghara* can also be used for leverage when mounting a female. Gharials are gregarious and operate within a strict social hierarchy – only the top-ranking males are permitted to mate.

Gharials are only found in the fast-flowing stretches of the Ganges and Brahmaputra systems with an isolated population in the Mahanadi River of Orissa, where sandy banks provide ideal conditions for egg-laying once the rivers have receded after the monsoon. The female gharial buries her eggs in the sand and guards the nest day and night for two months. By May, when the Ganges is at its lowest and the early summer sun has turned the sandbanks into natural incubators, the eggs are ready to hatch and the mother must dig them up.

The timing of this operation is crucial. The tiny crocodiles will not survive if they hatch while still buried in the sand; but the eggs are vulnerable to predation if the mother digs them up too soon. Crocodile babies have evolved a way of dealing with this problem: still inside their shells, the young give a cry to alert their mother to the fact that they are 'ready'; as she approaches and begins to dig up the eggs, the cries turn into a frantic chorus.

Gharials are born with a sharp bony horn on their snout, known as the egg tooth. It acts like a tin opener, enabling them to slice through the inner membrane of the egg and crack the outer shell. The young are tiny and immensely vulnerable. Their mother watches over her brood closely and, as soon as she can, moves them from the nest to the comparative safety of the river margin. Here, other newborns from the same group will be gathered, for gharial breeding is concentrated on this most propitious time of year and the mothers will share responsibility for guarding the crèche until the young are able to fend for themselves.

Like others of the crocodile family, gharials have evolved sophisticated techniques for controlling their body temperature. During cold winter nights they remain in the water at temperatures of 10–15°C. This is not warm enough to enable them to digest food, so they tend to stop feeding. During the day they bask in the sun and store the heat absorbed in the core of their body. This 'storage heating' is necessary for survival, particularly when temperatures drop. Although I have observed them at temperatures of 2°C, few gharials can survive for long periods below 10°C. The dominant members of the hierarchy assert their rights to the best basking sites; consequently, every 'basker' has its own niche.

In all there are probably 25,000 crocodiles in the wild in India and three of the world's 22 species are represented, the other two being the mugger or marsh crocodile and the saltwater crocodile. The latter grows up to 9 metres in length and is found from the mangrove forests of the Sundarbans on the India/Bangladesh border to the rivers

The gharial or gavial is now on course to recovery: its population has increased over the last two decades from a few hundred to several thousand.

OVERLEAF *The marsh crocodile or mugger races into a patch of water disturbing hundreds of cormorants and egrets.*

A marsh crocodile attacks a sambar fawn at the edge of a lake in Ranthambhore National Park.

of Sri Lanka and as far east as the Andaman and Nicobar Islands, 1500 kilometres across the Bay of Bengal towards Myanmar. Normally feeding on fish or small animals, it has been known to take goats and cattle as well.

The marsh crocodile is much smaller, growing to only about 3 metres, but is an extremely adaptable creature, at home in both Sri Lanka and Nepal as well as through-out India, and capable of surviving in a vast lake or a tiny stream. In the lakes of Ranthambhore National Park in Rajasthan I have observed violent clashes between tiger and marsh crocodiles over food. There, the crocodiles regularly killed the fawns of sambar, the large Indian deer which can often be seen in the waters of the lake, where it feeds on the juicy water vegetation.

In March 1984, a male tiger, whom we called Genghis, began to exploit the sambar's predilection for water, and over the summer months he killed some two dozen deer in the water. Killing an adult sambar on dry land, never mind in the water, is quite an achievement for a tiger, as a stag may weigh as much as 200 kilogrammes – about the same as a medium-sized male tiger and rather more than the average female. In addition to making his own kills, Genghis would ruthlessly scavenge anything he could from the crocodiles. He would pound through the water and, amid much snarling and hissing, push the crocodiles away from the carcass on which they had been feeding and drag it to the shore.

Because of the intense concentration of sambar on the fringes of the lake, natural deaths also occurred. The crocodiles would either pull carcasses into the water or guard them around the shallow edges of the lake. Since the sambar is so big, decomposition took some time and sooner or later Genghis would arrive on the scene.

On one such occasion, we found him sitting at the edge of the lake looking carefully at a spot in the water where some crocodiles were splashing and nibbling around what appeared to be the remains of an adult sambar. During the next couple of hours, he twice swam into the water, but failed to displace the crocodiles from their kill. Then he swam towards them a third time, smashing furiously at the water with his forepaws to frighten the crocodiles away. Dipping his head down he finally grabbed the carcass, which was bloated and stiff, and made for the shore. With one forepaw wrapped around the neck of the sambar and using the other to stroke through the water, he swam about 50 metres. Once, briefly, he went completely under. Eventually, he reached the safety of the tall grass on the shore and feasted undisturbed. Some fourteen years later this interaction between tigers and crocodiles continues in Ranthambhore's lakes.

The Brahmaputra

We have seen the place where Mother Ganga, the river Ganges, is born, and somewhere deep in the eastern Himalayas up on the Tibetan plateau, another mountain torrent created another great river. In the highlands of southeastern Tibet, the Yarlung Tsangpo River makes a U-turn and becomes the raging Brahmaputra. From this point the river flows westwards through Assam, before turning south through Bangladesh. In the course of its journey it creates lush wildlife habitat that compares with that of the Gangetic Plain.

Towards the end of the year, once the floodwaters of the Ganges and Brahmaputra have receded and the grassy plains are once more exposed, the megafauna return from the high ground where they have retreated during the monsoon. Here on the plains, from about November onwards, they eat and mate. One of the best places to observe them is Kaziranga National Park, in the far northeastern province of Assam. The annual flooding of the Brahmaputra has produced rich grassland that is home to some 1200

Indian one-horned rhinos – half of the world's wild population of this species. There was a time early this century when the population sank as low as twelve. The dramatic recovery has occurred because of the protection given to the rich grasslands.

The sweep of grassland is interrupted by pockets of semi-evergreen forest, deep, dark and dense, with luxuriant stands of cane. Around the edges tigers, dense in number, stalk their prey. Here, too, open-billed storks, black-necked and white-necked storks, adjutant storks, spotbills, teals and hundreds of grey-headed and Pallas fishing eagles all feast on fish. Some notes from my diary will give an idea of the atmosphere and of the wealth of wildlife to be found here:

> I am sitting atop a watchtower on Bahubil in Kaziranga. At the edge of the water a group of 20 pelicans fish furiously from one side to the other. On the far side I see ten otters scampering across the land into the water; with heads bobbing up and down they start to fish. Overhead a grey-headed fishing eagle swoops into the water and comes out with a 3-kilogramme fish caught firmly in its talons. A lesser adjutant stork spears another fish in the shallow water. Suddenly, on the far side, the grass moves and out come a female rhino and her calf. They look around and immerse themselves in the shallow water. I scan the far horizon with my binoculars and discover three hog deer grazing in the grass, and further afield a group of swamp deer. A herd of wild buffalo are busy grazing the edges of the water. Four of them settle down near the bank. A vast bull walks menacingly towards a younger animal. It is probably a scene unchanged for hundreds of years.
>
> The quiet of the evening is shattered by the sharp alarm calls of the hog deer. I scan the grass hoping for the magical appearance of a tiger, but I can't spot a stripe. At dusk a large tusker appears and enters the water in an effort to wallow, and attempts a bottoms-up posture as he sinks his tusks into the mud. Again, alarm calls resound and I have visions of a tiger attacking a buffalo. A forest guard whispers in my ear that when the pelicans come to nest, the tiger waits nearby, and if the chicks fall he gobbles them up. Tiger eating pelican! What an image that conjures up.

A few months later, from the Bahubil tower, I had the extraordinary luck to witness an enormous tiger being chased first by a rhino and then by a wild buffalo. Later in the afternoon the tiger stalked a group of hog deer, unsuccessfully. But I had encountered the great giants of Kaziranga interacting, and it was for me like a dream come true.

A one-horned rhinoceros with her calf in the flood-plains of Kaziranga National Park.
The waters of the Brahmaputra River inundate the park each year, forcing the wildlife
to find refuge on high ground.

OVERLEAF *Thousands of pelicans exploit the rich flood-plains*
of the Brahmaputra to live in and rear their young.

Today, Kaziranga is home to a thriving tiger population. Dr Ullas Karanth, a scientist studying tiger densities, believes that the park can boast the highest density in India: nearly seventeen tigers to every hundred square kilometres. A number of giants – rhinos, elephants, wild buffalo and gaur (wild oxen) – also share this land with countless hog deer, swamp deer, sambar deer and much else. The park seems to me a veritable Noah's Ark: lesser and greater pied hornbills screech through the air, turtles bask in the sun, otters race across large sheets of water, competing with thousands of pelicans for the vast amounts of fish, rhinos stand as if transported from some prehistoric age, and swamp partridges strut around the edge of the grass.

Pockets of forest within the grasslands are a frenzy of greens, as all that grows is coiled, looped and encircled in an endless embrace. Red jungle fowl streak across the entangled foliage and orchids sprout from the branches in flashes of magenta and pink. Giant animals have made so many paths through the grasslands that the smaller herbivores have few problems in finding grazing pastures. Here is a true network of life, a food chain that has been alive for centuries. If you remove one species, there may be real problems for another. In the hilly forests nearby there are still troops of hoolock gibbons and capped langurs, and some say there could even be the elusive clouded leopard. In between the forest and grasslands is an array of birds, including emerald doves, imperial pigeons and kingfishers. I spent eight hours driving through this forest and lost count of rhinos after reaching 100. Alongside were plenty of elephants and wild buffaloes. As the sun sets and darkness falls, the grass comes alive with the glow of fireflies. They look like a blanket of light that ignites the night.

The web of grassland, woodland, cane, lake and river survives in Kaziranga thanks to the dedication of the armed forest guards who live for six months of the year in this watery habitat and protect the area from the constant onslaughts of poachers. Guard posts are built on stilts because of the floods, and each has a cat to deal with the rats. Each post also has a shrine to the goddess Durga and her vehicle, the tiger. On special days, and before and after a patrol, the forest guards seek her blessing and protection in their anti-poaching endeavours. They spend most of their time patrolling the wet grasslands in search of poachers and are ever alert for the sound of gunfire. Every year gun battles with poachers rage, and many of these guards have sacrificed their lives to protect Kaziranga. They told me that, at the height of the floods, snakes climb into the guard posts for safety, and man and snake live together, knowing that neither will attack the

A patch of semi-evergreen riverine forest in Assam's Kaziranga National Park.
Small pockets of riverine forest are scattered across the flood-plains.

other. Similarly, other animals, often adversaries, abide together peacefully on higher ground, all waiting for the water to recede.

At the edges of the Brahmaputra the receding waters create great islands of grass that become breeding grounds for floricans, hog deer and swamp deer. This is also where the tiger stalks and kills. Many factors contribute to the area's natural wealth: floods bring nutrients that enrich the soil, multitudes of fish fill the waters, man-made fires burn the grasses and create lush new growth, and animal movement to higher ground during floods allows the grass on the flood-plains to renew itself. This cycle of life supports high densities of predator and prey populations.

Although the tiger is the dominant predator throughout the subcontinent, in these grasslands it sometimes comes into conflict with the giant herbivores. Great battles are fought between tigers and wild buffaloes. Tigers have been known to prey successfully on buffaloes – which are huge creatures, weighing up to 900 kilogrammes – but there have also been cases of tigers being gored to death by buffalo and rhino.

One morning at dawn – and in the northeastern part of the subcontinent it comes very early – I suddenly confront a rhino, who wheels around to charge the jeep. The rhinos in these grasslands are aggressive and, like the elephants, do not tolerate human beings in close proximity. Fortunately, this rhino changes its mind and veers off into the undergrowth.

Cave paintings in central India, which date back 10,000 years, prove that rhinos have existed in the subcontinent for a very long time. The Indus Valley civilizations documented them 5000 years ago, and there are records of hunts on the frontiers of Kashmir in the fourteenth century. It was about 500 years ago that the great river basins created the pockets of grassland and expanses of water which are essential for their survival. At that time the Indian subcontinent could boast all three Asiatic species of rhino: the Javan rhino, the Sumatran two-horned rhino and the great one-horned rhino. Today, only the last survives – in tiny pockets in the east of India and parts of Nepal, where once it was spread across the entire Gangetic Plain.

Folklore and superstition surround the rhino, from the medicinal and aphrodisiacal properties of its horns to the magical qualities of its flesh and blood. Rhino urine is considered a vital antiseptic and is also believed to act as a charm against ghosts and evil spirits. Keepers in various Indian zoos have been offered large sums of money by visitors to wet handkerchiefs in rhino urine for use in various cures! Unfortunately, the high value placed on rhino products has led to the decimation of the animals by poachers across the Indian subcontinent and throughout Southeast Asia.

Prehistoric in appearance and seemingly armour-plated like a tank, these rhinos require a lot of serious eating and rumination to keep them going. Studies of their

Giant herbifauna like the one-horned rhinoceros are now restricted to a few small pockets along the Brahmaputra flood-plains and the Nepalese terai.

feeding habits have discovered that they feed on nearly 200 species of plants from over 50 botanical families. The presence of the rhino reflects the health and diversity of the grasslands.

Adult rhinos are solitary, with both sexes living within a territory and coming together only to mate. Males tend to be more exclusive about their ranges than females. They mark them out by spraying strategic points with urine, which they can squirt over distances of 4 metres. They also rub their horns on bushes, make parallel furrows by dragging their hind legs on the ground, and defecate at significant spots to discourage potential intruders.

During mating the bull becomes highly aggressive; conflicts between male and female are common. Bulls also use their sharp teeth to inflict serious wounds on other males and have been known to kill solitary young males whom they presumably regard as rivals. The rhino's thick skin offers some protection from injury, but it is not impenetrable: despite its appearance, it can actually be quite soft.

Females come into oestrus at any time of the year. Copulation can last an hour or two, during which time the bull will ejaculate fifty or sixty times. The female has to bear the 2-tonne weight of the bull and there have been cases of young females dying from spinal injuries sustained during mating. Females have their first calf around the age of seven, and thereafter can give birth every three years. Calves are born throughout the year, and although weaned in twelve months, continue to live with their mother for three to four years, often until just before the birth of the next calf. Independence is acquired gradually, a few days at a time, until the calf leaves for good. Tigers in Kaziranga regularly kill rhino calves – up to eight such deaths a year have been recorded – but suffer the wrath of the mothers in return.

Adult rhinos look superficially alike, but males are larger and have a thicker horn, often with the tip broken. A keen observer can recognize individual rhinos by variations in horn and ear shape, or by cuts, scars and other irregularities in the folds of their bodies.

Wild buffaloes

Another giant of the grasslands is the wild buffalo, which can stand 2 metres at the shoulder, weigh more than a tonne and have horns over 1 metre long and 2.5 metres wide. Once distributed across the large rivers and their tributaries in the Gangetic Plain and right up to the flood-plains of Assam, the buffalo is now found only in small parts of Assam and in Bastar, central India. There are also small populations in parts of Nepal where the grasslands are relatively undisturbed. The total population does not exceed 2000.

Reed brakes, grass plains and swampy land are the buffalo's ideal habitats. It can spend hours lying on the banks of a river before submerging itself in the water. It ranges over a wide area, travelling long distances while grazing.

The buffalo's rutting period starts late in the autumn and continues into the new year. Bulls tend to be solitary, associating with a herd of females and sub-adult males only when a female is in oestrus. Then males may clash viciously over the female in question. Both males and females, although shy of human beings, can be aggressive towards intruders. If the calves are approached by predators, especially tigers, their mothers form a protective front. Buffaloes frequently snort and stamp if threatened, but can attack viciously if suddenly confronted. They have certainly been known to kill tigers, charge rhinos and chase elephants. They also gore to death several human intruders each year.

I once spent an hour sitting atop an elephant watching rhinos, buffaloes, swamp deer, boars and hog deer enjoying the water. On top of one giant you can get very close to others, without fear of reprisal, particularly if they all like to wallow. The mud protects their skins from the burning sun and biting insects.

The wild buffalo attacks without provocation and has on many occasions
even chased away tigers.

Hog deer and swamp deer

If the existence of rhinos indicates the health of the habitat, so does the presence of hog deer (*para*) and swamp deer (*barasingha*), two other residents of these lush grasslands. The hog deer is distributed right across the grass plains from west to east and into Myanmar, favouring riverine tracts, open grasslands and river islands where the grass is not too high. Hundreds of thousands once roamed the flood-plains and *terai*, but as the habitat fragmented due to agricultural encroachment, populations declined sharply.

Stout, speckled and brown-coated, the hog deer stands barely 60 centimetres at the shoulder. It probably gets its name from its squat, rotund shape and the way it holds its head very low like a pig. It also moves with a rather lumbering, porcine gait. It is generally solitary, although a pair may frequent the same spot for long periods and in Manas Sanctuary on the India / Bhutan border in Assam thousands have been known to congregate together. Wary, alert and nervous, it has a high-pitched alarm call which warns others of the presence of predators.

I have spent long hours observing these deer, from Corbett National Park in the western foothills of Uttar Pradesh to Manas in the east. I believe that their pastures are created by the grazing habits of elephants, rhinos, wild buffaloes and even gaur, and that their survival is linked to the survival of these large animals. Small herbivores follow in the steps of giant herbivores. Where the elephant population has suffered a sharp decline and the rhino has become extinct, as in Dudhwa, the grass may grow so high that small herbivores find it impossible to graze. Consequently, populations of animals such as the hog deer and swamp deer have rapidly declined. There are now fewer than 5000 swamp deer left in the wild.

Being primarily grassland animals, swamp deer move away from their favoured habitat only when the water rises on the flood-plains. At that time much feasting is done in adjacent crop fields.

There are three subspecies of swamp deer, one found in the grasslands and forests near the India / Nepal border, another in the swamps of the *terai* and Assam, and the third further south on the hard, open ground in Madhya Pradesh. Specially adapted to alluvial grasslands, they are highly gregarious – a few kilometres of swamp can contain hundreds of individuals. A dominant stag with well-developed antlers commands a herd of females and young. Other adult males form 'stag parties' or bachelor groups.

The onset of winter brings the rut, and rutting stags are frequently found wallowing in the swamps, uttering hoarse braying calls. There is little serious conflict between adult males – the dominant stag attains and defends his position more by posturing than by fighting. One means of achieving this end is to cover his antlers with tussocks of grass to make them look even more impressive. They are already startling enough – the name *barasingha* means 'twelve horns', and a male's antlers have at least twelve prongs.

This is a good time for the females to be pregnant. The grass is growing tall and lush in the newly drained swamps, and the cool weather means there are fewer biting flies to pester them. As spring comes and temperatures rise, the males shed their antlers and both sexes lose their long winter coat, in preparation for the hot summer to come. The young are born in the spring and hidden among the long grass; had they been born at the height of the monsoon they would have been vulnerable to predation by crocodiles. But their future survival is dependent on how effectively we protect their surroundings. Every year, under enormous pressure from agriculture, some of this habitat vanishes.

Manas

A few hundred kilometres further down the Brahmaputra from Kaziranga is another unique ecological system. Home to twenty-two of the subcontinent's fifty-four endangered species, Manas Sanctuary and Tiger Reserve must be one of India's most productive grasslands, interspersed with some of the finest riverine tracts of both moist deciduous and semi-evergreen forest. However, the area is under constant assault from poachers, timber mafias, armed political insurgents, who take shelter in it, and encroachers, who have pillaged one of the world's finest natural treasures.

Manas nestles below the foothills of the Bhutan Himalayas and derives its name from the river that rushes through it. Immediately across the border in Bhutan lies Manas Wildlife Sanctuary. Together the two parks provide over 3000 square kilometres of protected area: the Bhutanese sanctuary is the oldest in the country, while the core of the Indian sanctuary coming under the auspices of Project Tiger.

The beauty of the place silences me. It is another Noah's Ark, with rhinos, elephants, wild buffaloes, gaur, sambar, chital, swamp deer, barking deer, hog deer, hundreds of greater pied hornbills, florican, the endemic pygmy hog, hispid hare and golden langur, plus cloud leopards and golden cats. This is an even greater variety of herbivores than found in Kaziranga. Here in the foothills, the Himalayas encircle you just before the flood-plains start, and late in the evening a whispering breeze turns into a raging wind that howls through the night. Vast bombax trees reach for the sky and elephant flies sweep in to strike. The geckos are enormous and at night make a din that is hard to forget.

OVERLEAF *Typical to the* terai *and the flood-plains of India are the hog deer and the giant elephant grass which they inhabit. They can only enter these patches of high grass when larger herbivores have made paths into them.*

Endemic species thrive here. The pygmy hog is the smallest wild pig in the world – about 60 centimetres long and no more than 30 centimetres high at the shoulder. Because of its size and grassland habitat it is very difficult to observe. Said to be extinct in 1958, it was later rediscovered in Manas and on the Paaniri Tea Estate in Assam. It has small hairless ears and the male has short tusks. Diurnal in habit, it is known to eat birds, monitor lizards, insects, roots and tubers. Adults are solitary and the sexes interact only during the mating season, when aggression over courtship is frequent. A litter may consist of from two to six piglets, each smaller than the palm of a hand.

Even less is documented about the elusive hispid hare, otherwise known as the Assam rabbit. In fact it is neither a true rabbit nor a true hare, belonging to the genus *Caprolagus*. It is about the same size as a hare, with coarse dark brown fur on its back, lighter brown fur on its belly and a short brown tail. It has long claws and large teeth which enable it to feed mainly on bark and roots.

Unfortunately, both these species have almost vanished as grasslands have been burnt and converted for agriculture. Floods in the Brahmaputra basin have swept away

The rare and endangered pygmy hogs are restricted to parts of northern Assam, their last refuge in the world.

RIGHT *An elephant crosses the Manas River on the border of India and Bhutan. These riverine forests are a World Heritage site.*

many of these forest pygmies. Those that survive have further enemies in birds of prey and other predators of the grasslands, including man. They are engaged in a continuous battle for survival.

However, size alone is no guarantee of safety; even the elephant faces extinction within these fragile and vanishing grasslands. The fate of Manas and of all the wildlife that depends on it lies in our hands. We must take immediate decisions to ensure that these tracts of forest and grassland are kept inviolate – if not, they will gradually disappear and may be gone by the turn of the century.

The mangrove swamps of the Sundarbans

So, having travelled some way down the Ganges, then across to the Brahmaputra, we reach the northern tip of the cone-shaped Bay of Bengal, where the Ganges, Brahmaputra and Meghna rivers merge to create a delta that extends over 80,000 square kilometres. Fringing it and stretching across the border between India and Bangladesh is the swampy region known as the Sundarbans, which encompasses probably the largest tract of mangroves in the world. Here the melting snows that have gushed through the plains meet the sea. Some 70 per cent of the land at this junction is flooded every day, and all the fauna retreat to higher ground, following the movement of the tides.

The islands of the Sundarbans have been formed from silt deposits carried down from the Himalayas by rivers – a simple enough procedure which has created a unique ecological system. A maze of waterways weaves through 10,000 square kilometres of silt-loaded islands whose impenetrability makes them a true haven for wildlife. An early description of the area comes from François Bernier, a Frenchman who explored these swamps between 1656 and 1668:

…the most striking and peculiar beauty of Bengale [sic] is the innumerable islands filling the vast space between the two banks of the Ganges, in some places six or seven days' journey asunder. These islands vary in size, but are all extremely fertile, surrounded with wood, and abounding in fruit-trees, and pine-apples, and covered with verdure; a thousand water-channels run through them, stretching beyond the sight, and resembling long walks arched with trees… In traversing the Ganges in small rowing boats, the usual mode of conveyance among these islands, it is in many places dangerous to land, and great care must be had that the boat, which during the night is fastened to a tree, be kept at some distance from the shore, for it constantly happens that some person or another falls a prey to tigers. These ferocious animals are very apt, it is said, to enter into the boat itself, while the people are asleep, and to carry away some victim, who, if we are to believe the boatmen of the country, generally happens to be the stoutest and fattest of the party.

In the evening of the fourth day we withdrew, as usual, out of the main channel to a place of security, and passed a most extraordinary night. Not a breath of wind was felt, and the air became so hot and suffocating that we could scarcely breathe. The bushes around us were so full of glow-worms that they seemed ignited; and fires resembling flames arose every moment to the great alarm of our sailors, who did not doubt that they were so many devils…

The first day we ascended a narrow canal of stagnant water, winding between low, marshy islands, covered with thick jungle, above which a few cocoa-trees, with their immense plume-like foliage loaded with fruit, rose like rockets into the air. The banks of the canal were hidden by an inextricable maze of roots and aquatic plants, rendering them almost unapproachable. Flocks of birds peopled these fetid shores, and amongst them I distinguished the giant heron, the large black stork, the arghilah, and the brown ibis… The water itself in certain places was covered by hundreds of little divers and Brahmin ducks; and water-fowl, with purple or indigo-tinted plumage, darted over the lotus-leaves. I shot a few; but each time, before we could approach them, the bird suddenly disappeared, drawn beneath the water by an invisible power. These game-stealers were no other than the crocodiles which swarm in these waters, but which, alarmed by the reports of our guns, prudently hid under the surface.

Crocodiles are not the only enemies against which the inhabitants of the Sundarbans have to defend their wretched existence. The jungles which surround them on every side abound in wild beasts of every kind; but tigers especially are there in prodigious numbers. These animals swim easily from one island to another, and sometimes they make a concerted attack upon the villagers, who are then compelled to surround their dwelling with palisades and sustain a regular siege.

Today much of the habitat has changed and many of the tigers have been slaughtered, but the Sundarbans remain magical. It is one of the most important mangrove forests in the world. I travelled 150 kilometres of waterways through thick mangrove, searching

OVERLEAF *The mangrove forests of the Sundarbans extend across the border of India and Bangladesh. Highly inaccessible, this region is home to one of the largest remaining populations of tigers.*

111

for the stripes I never saw, but the presence of the tiger creates a powerful atmosphere. It is everywhere but you do not see it. Its pugmarks on the mudbanks reveal the slippery footholds it negotiates as it moves from land to water and water to land. Here I watched Gangetic dolphins in the rivers, saltwater crocodiles basking in the sun and six different kingfishers diving for their prey. Spotted deer (*chital*) and wild boar graze on the edges of the swamps and the waters are full of fish, crabs, lobsters and so much natural wealth that hundreds of fishing boats brimming with their catches seem not to deplete it.

When the waters recede, many mammals and birds come to the humid mud-flats to devour the protein-rich marine life left behind. The rhesus macaques who feed on the fruit of the mangrove are messy eaters and the white spotted deer (*chital*) congregate below to feast on what the monkeys drop. At the same time, the macaques act as a lookout and warn against approaching predators. As the chital browse and clear the lower levels of the mangrove forests, the macaques are able to descend and hunt the crabs on the swamp floor – and at this low level the deer prove the better lookouts. Fishing cats scoop up fish with their paws and monitor lizards scavenge what they can, fighting over dead fish.

Over the centuries the animals that inhabit the Sundarbans have evolved in many different ways in order to cope with life in a mangrove swamp. Aquatic reptiles have flattened tails to facilitate wriggling; mudskipper fish breathe through their skin and use their pelvic fins to climb trees, thus escaping the tides; fiddler crabs change colour

A mudskipper rests on a mangrove root in the Sundarbans.

with the tides, and survive on land by retaining water in their gills and 'frothing' it to create oxygen. Wild boars eat dead fish, molluscs and sea-turtle eggs; spotted deer secrete excess salt from salt water through their glands; even snakes have adapted to hunting in mud and water. The mud-flats of the Sundarbans are home to millions of burrowing worms, and thriving populations of shrimp live in the saltier expanses nearer the sea.

In this low-lying country mangroves are as much the 'tree of life' as the fig tree is in the tropical forest. Of the fifty true mangrove species in the world, as many as twenty-six are found in the Sundarbans. Submerged twice a day by the incoming tides they act as buffers to reduce the incursion of the sea; they prevent cyclonic weather by controlling the impact of wind and water; through capillary action and chemical exchange they even reduce the salinity of the ground water. Decayed plants, rotted by the warm, wet environment, feed a rich and diverse planktonic life on which both crabs and fish thrive. Mangrove trees and shrubs help to anchor the mud – no easy task since it is always shifting.

In conditions under which most plants would be smothered, mangroves have had to adapt. Their systems of prop roots grow to considerable widths to overcome the physical instability of the wet, clay soil. They have had to become tolerant of salt. Their thick, waxy, leathery leaves conserve fresh water whenever it rains, but also contain salt glands, which excrete excess salt from the sea water on which they depend for much of the year. Although the mud in which they grow is very rich, it contains no oxygen,

Fiddler crabs out on the shore of an island in the Ganges delta in search of food.

A water monitor absorbs the sun's warmth amid the varied mangrove ecosystem.

so mangroves have developed a spongy tissue on their bark, enabling them to draw oxygen directly from the air. Some of their roots grow up through the mud, creating a carpet of sharp spikes which also absorb oxygen.

Mangroves produce long, thin, pointed seeds which hang downwards and sprout while still attached to the parent plant. Once the shoots are large enough, the seed drops vertically, pointed end down, and the momentum of the fall is sufficient to enable it to spear itself in the mud. As the seedling grows, it uses its parent's prop roots to support itself.

Left to themselves, mangroves spread rapidly and in the Sundarbans they continue to colonize new islands which emerge on their seaward margin. On the landward side, however, they are under pressure as other demands are made on the land and the trees themselves are chopped down for charcoal. The governments of both India and Bangladesh are making efforts to conserve the mangrove forests as a vital tiger habitat.

Although there are many fewer tigers than there were in François Bernier's day, the population in the Sundarbans is one of the largest surviving in the world – about 600-700. Living as they do amid a constantly changing network of channels up to 2 kilometres wide, the Sundarban tigers have become powerful swimmers, living almost equally happily in water as on land. A tiger has been seen swimming 8 kilometres from the shore. They have learned to eat fish and crabs and to drink salt water. But when the tide is high and vast areas of the delta inundated, they must guard against the saltwater crocodile, as this large reptile competes with them for prey.

The Sundarbans are very heavily populated: some half a million people depend directly or indirectly on the livelihood they can glean from the forest and the swamps. They are allowed into the forest only to collect wood or honey, and can fish only with a licence. But all these activities bring them into conflict with the tigers who hunt in the same diminishing habitats. Tigers used to take a toll of at least thirty to forty people a year. Today, due to better management of human movement, the figure is down to three people a year. This is largely due to low visibility, which means that men and tigers stumble upon each other accidentally. In the resulting confrontations, men invariably come off worse.

Little wonder, then, that local villages seek protection by worshipping the tiger god. In this area villagers turn to the Hindu goddess Banobibi, mother of the forest, and her Muslim consort Dakshin Rai, making an intriguing link between the two religions. Few people set off into the tiger's territory without making an offering to Banobibi's shrine: her blessings protect people from the tiger's anger. But it is Dakshin Rai who is regarded as the supreme ruler of the Sundarbans, lord of all things whether ghosts or demons, crocodiles or tigers. He is depicted riding on the tiger's back, and his ability to enter the body of the tiger is legendary. Banobibi is offered rice, fruits, sweets and flowers, while Dakshin Rai attracts musicians, who perform with sacred drums around his image. The shrine at Sajnekhali in the Sundarbans is visited regularly by the people of more than fifty villages, and Banobibi and Dakshin Rai are vociferously propitiated.

The people of the Sundarbans and Assam have forged another close relationship with a wild creature, though this is a practical rather than a mystical one. They have trained the Indian smooth-coated otter to fish for them. Otters are naturally expert fishers, so are often persecuted in areas where the local people earn their livelihood through fishing. In the wild otters fish co-operatively; even a family of eight – two adults, four subadults, and two young pups – can work together. They swim in a line, then at a signal that is invisible to human observers they all dive together. Most other species of otter are sight hunters, so this communal activity may be an adaptation to the silty waters in which they live.

In the Sundarbans otters are bred in captivity. Adults are tethered to the fishing boat with plaited hessian cords tied round their middle, then sent into the water. This exploitation of an animal by man is quite cruel, as this naturally free-ranging creature is tamed and made to perform much like a dog on a chain. Over many centuries, the largest land mammal, the elephant, has also been snatched from the wild and tamed to move at man's command. The same is true of the cheetah: extinct on the subcontinent today, it was once chained to a leash and trained to hunt the black buck across the grasslands of India.

Dakshin Rai on his vehicle, the tiger, is regarded as the supreme ruler of the Sundarbans mangrove forests. He is the lord of all things, be it ghosts or demons, crocodiles or tigers.

Short-clawed otters are the expert fishermen of these waters.

Here the otters fish for themselves, but in so doing flush out fish hiding in the nearby reeds and send them towards the fishing nets. These are large structures held in place underwater with a boom, so that the fish cannot escape by swimming downwards. Using this method the humans catch many more fish than they would otherwise expect, and the otters, though chained, remain well fed.

Young otters participate in these fishing trips but are not tethered. They are free to swim where they like, but return instinctively to their parents, just as they would in the wild. However, their freedom lasts for only a short period in their lives.

The Sundarbans are a tiger fortress by the sea, a frontier between land and sea where rivers meet and merge into salt water. Beyond these mangroves are the vast oceans that wash the subcontinent's shores – a world of blue and green water and beautiful coral sands. Another journey begins.

OVERLEAF   *The Sundarbans tiger is a great swimmer, moving from one island*
to another and slipping in and out of the water with great agility.
Its life in these mangrove forests is unknown to man.

CHAPTER THREE

OCEANS AND ISLANDS

THE MOON IS RISING behind me as I stare across the vast black ocean. Nearby a white beach glints in the moonlight. The sound of waves crashing on the shore reminds me that I am on the eastern coast of India, in the state of Orissa, looking out over the Bay of Bengal. I have seen this sea before, from the mangrove swamps of the Sundarbans, to the northeast of here, and I am reminded again that the forests act like giant sponges, absorbing rain, then slowly squeezing it into streams and rivers, which finally end their journey in the vast oceans.

Now it is *arribada*, or nesting time, and the sight that confronts me here on a beach on the coast of Orissa, is startling. Thousands of female olive Ridley turtles are emerging like an army from the waves. Each one will find a spot to dig and lay her eggs. Tonight more than a million eggs will be laid, then the turtle army will vanish into the sea again. In a few months' time hundreds of thousands of young will hatch and, like their parents, they will disappear into the Bay of Bengal, only to return years later to lay their own eggs.

This is the largest breeding colony of sea turtles in the world and no one knows for certain why they choose this particular 10-kilometre stretch of sand. The only other places where olive Ridleys breed in profusion are on the beaches of Mexico and Costa Rica. Sea turtles are almost completely aquatic. It seems unlikely that males ever come ashore at all; certainly mating takes place in the open sea. The only time the female ventures on to land is when she walks 30 metres or so from the water's edge to lay her eggs. Although she is slow, clumsy and vulnerable on land, she needs to go this far to be sure that even the highest tides cannot drown her eggs. She uses her flippers to dig a pit in the sand, where she lays 100–150 eggs at a time. When she has finished, she covers the pit with sand and smacks her bulk on it to pack it down.

Bottle-nose dolphins with their great agility leap out of the ocean as if flying. Of the world's twenty-eight dolphin species, sixteen live in the Indo-Malayan seas.

For the next 60–75 days the eggs are left to look after themselves some 40–45 centimetres below the sand. Once hatched, the young remain covered by 5–10 centimetres of sand for three days, then they begin their rush to the sea as birds, crabs and other predators swoop in to feast. Thousands die before reaching the water, but many more make it. Even so, they have to swim frantically for the first two days until they are beyond reach of the shoreline predators.

Thereafter, we know very little of the life of these tiny turtles until they reach adulthood, by which time they will have grown to a length of 80 centimetres and weigh 60–75 kilogrammes. Experts differ on how long this takes: some say ten or twelve years, others as many as twenty-five or even thirty. Then the adult females return to the same beach to nest: an extraordinary feat of navigation, as sea turtles have been observed 4000 kilometres away from their breeding grounds. In a lifespan of 70–75 years a female turtle could lay 3000–5000 eggs. On this single stretch of beach 50 million eggs are laid each year. However, scientists believe that only 1 per cent of these reach adulthood.

The coastal waters of India are home to four other species of sea turtle: leatherback, green, hawksbill and loggerhead. The first three are known to nest at various sites along the Indian coast, as well as in the Lakshadweep Islands and the Andaman and Nicobar Islands, which we shall visit later. The leatherback is the largest, growing up to 2 metres, and is adapted to both temperate and tropical waters, migrating even further than the olive Ridley. Like the olive Ridley, the green sea turtle is confined to the tropics. The hawksbill is most frequently seen near coral reefs. Little is known of the habits of the loggerhead turtle, but it probably breeds in subtropical waters, reaching the coasts of India only occasionally.

All five species are fast and agile swimmers. They differ from tortoises and freshwater terrapins in that they cannot withdraw their head and limbs into their shell. They also lack teeth, but their sharp jaws can crush and tear food.

Fishermen around India's coastline revere the turtle as a reincarnation of the Hindu god Vishnu, and sculptured turtles are worshipped in coastal temples. With its slow, steady gait the turtle is a symbol of perseverance, and revered for its ability to carry heavy burdens. However, the increase in industrial-scale fishing off the Indian coast and the pollution that this brings, plus a growing trade in turtle meat, means that all five of these species are on the endangered list.

Down the east coast

A little further down Orissa's eastern coast lies Chilika Lake, actually an estuarine lagoon near the mouth of the River Daya, covering an area of 1000 square kilometres and connected to the Bay of Bengal by a channel nearly 29 kilometres long. Formed

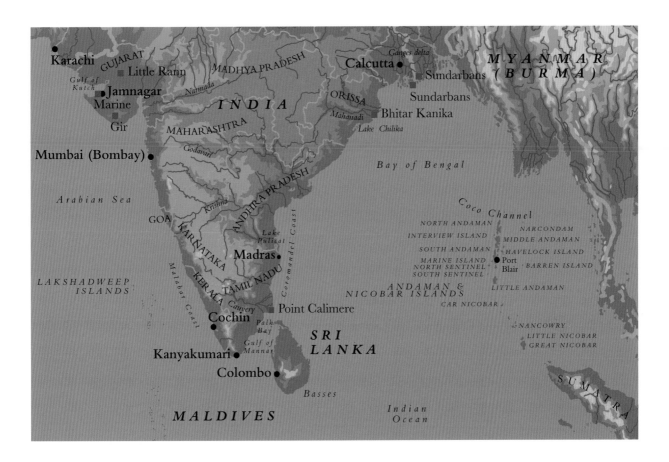

probably about 8000 years ago when rock lineaments fractured and allowed massive marine inundation, this shallow lagoon must be one of the subcontinent's finest wetlands.

To the west and south the lake is bounded by hills, while in the northeast is an extensive area of marshy land, some of which has been reclaimed for agriculture. Here sedgy banks and islands, formed each year from silt brought down by the rivers, peep just above the surface. The pear-shaped lake is some 70 kilometres long, and the narrow tidal stream which rushes through the channel connecting it to the sea keeps the water distinctly salty between December and June. After the monsoon, rainwaters rush in from the north, driving out the sea water. This cyclical variation of salinity creates a unique ecosystem in which both marine and estuarine species thrive.

The area is home to over 150 species of fish, 35 species of migratory birds and over 120 species of other birds. A rough estimate suggests that half a million birds visit the

OVERLEAF *Hundreds of thousands of olive Ridley turtles come ashore to lay their eggs. After over two months millions of young will be born and they will immediately take to the sea.*

Thousands of spotted redshanks at Point Calimere on their perpetual quest for food.

waters of Chilika in the winter, many of them nesting on the island of Nalbana in the middle of the lagoon.

The channel that connects Chilika to the sea is a favourite haunt of dolphins. Of the world's twenty-eight species, sixteen live in the Indo-Malayan seas. They vary enormously in shape and size: at one extreme they can be slim and streamlined, like the right whale dolphins, and at the other, squat and thick, like the blunt-nosed and stocky Risso's dolphin, which can reach a length of over 4 metres and weigh 680 kilo-grammes. Coastal dolphins occur in waters less than 30 metres deep, though some of them are capable of diving to depths of 600 metres to catch bottom-dwelling fish. They can eat 3–6 per cent of their body weight every day, primarily in fish.

Dolphins associate in groups of fewer than a hundred in coastal waters, but may congregate in several hundreds far offshore. Another large species of the Indian Ocean, bottle-nose dolphins begin breeding at the age of nine or ten and can live as long as thirty years. Calves are born after a gestation period of twelve months and suckle for up to eighteen months.

Moving south along the east coast from Orissa into Andhra Pradesh, there are more mangroves, coral reefs and wetlands. Further down, in the southern state of Tamil Nadu, the Vedaranyam salt swamps and Point Calimere lead us into the Gulf of Mannar and the Marine National Park.

Point Calimere is a low promontory at the edge of the sea, where, in the past, inland stretches of reserved forest housed much wildlife. It is also regarded as a sacred spot: a temple in the area is a place of pilgrimage, and many pilgrims bathe in the nearby ocean to wash away their sins. Being only 65 kilometres from Sri Lanka, Point Calimere is an important staging post in the movement of both resident and migratory birds. The peak of migration takes place in October and the salt-flats around the area support healthy populations of greater and lesser flamingoes.

Grey pelicans nest here too, feeding their ungainly but appealing chicks through an intriguing co-operative effort. A group of adults forms a semi-circle, splashing their wings vigorously to drive fish and crustaceans before them into the shallows. They then use their great pouches as fishing nets to scoop up the prey.

Off the coast of Sri Lanka

The island of Sri Lanka is nearly half the size of England: 435 kilometres long and 225 kilometres wide at its broadest point. The east coast is rugged, the palms of the south and west being replaced by scrub jungles. The centre of the broad southern end of the island consists of a mountain massif which covers 10,500 square kilometres and intercepts the rains of the monsoon. The mountains are a wet zone, used to rainfall of 500 centimetres a year, and the vegetation differs totally from that of the northern and eastern plains, which receive less than 125 centimetres of rain a year. The highest summit in the area is 2500 metres and, as we shall see in Chapter 5, equatorial rainforests dominate in the hill country. Open tracts of grassland, called *patanas*, occur in drier parts of the hilly regions, while rich grasslands thrive in the eastern lowlands. The muddy shores are fringed with mangrove swamps.

Sri Lanka is elephant country, and over three thousand of them roam the forests. Here, too, are leopards, four species of deer, three species of monkey, sloth bears, wild pigs, squirrels, otters, mongooses and over four hundred species of birds. A diversity of snakes, plus crocodiles, turtles and at least thirty-seven species of frogs and toads, add to the island's animal riches.

The shallow seas of the northwest are home to the rare dugong or sea cow, which comes to feed on a special seaweed that grows there. It is the dugong female's habit of sitting almost upright in the water while nursing her young in her flippers that gave

rise to stories of mermaids in these seas. The naturalist Stanley Prater, who was born and bred in India, described the origins of these beliefs in his article 'The Dugong or Sea Cow', published in *The Journal of the Bombay Natural History Society* (1928):

> The habit of rising half out of the water combined with the rude resemblance under these circumstances to a human being gave rise among earlier voyagers to India to stories of legendary beings, half human and half fish… Megasthenes records the existence of a creature in the ocean near Ceylon with the aspect of a woman, while the Portuguese and Spaniards gave the dugong a name signifying 'woman fish'. Again, the hairy lips of the dugong may, with a little imagination, have prompted Aelian's marvellous description of fishes with heads of lions, panthers and rams inhabiting the seas of Ceylon, for it is significant that the Dutch call the dugong the 'little bearded man'.

Dugongs are the sole surviving representatives of sea cows and grow to 3 metres long, weighing up to 500 kilogrammes and consuming over 20 kilogrammes of sea grass every day. Males are distinguished by having a pair of prominent incisors, while females have mammae (milk-secreting organs) near the armpit at the base of their flippers. Gestation can last for thirteen months and lactation continues for eighteen months, so female and offspring are very close. They have be known to live more than twenty years.

Dugongs are found not only in Sri Lanka, but also in the Gulf of Kutch and Mannar, Palk Bay, along the Malabar Coast and around the Andaman and Nicobar Islands, where the local people refer to them as the water pig. But they are now rarely seen in any of these places and as the shallow waters containing the sea grass on which they depend are under threat, their future is bleak.

The Andaman and Nicobar Islands

To the east of Sri Lanka, where the Bay of Bengal becomes the Andaman Sea, lies the isolated archipelago of the Andaman and Nicobar Islands. These are in fact the summits of a submerged mountain range and form a chain that extends for 800 kilometres.

LEFT *The endangered dugong or sea cow frequents the northeast coast of Sri Lanka. It has been regarded for years as the 'mermaid' of the sea.*

OVERLEAF *The Andaman and Nicobar islands are a part of a submerged mountain range that extends across 800 kilometres.*

Once part of the Asian mainland, they now lie some 1200 kilometres off the coast of Orissa, much closer to Myanmar and Indonesia than to India.

As in Sri Lanka, the geographic isolation of these islands has given rise to numerous endemic species of both flora and fauna. The tiny island of Narcondam, for example, believed to be a long-extinct craterless volcano no more than 5 square kilometres in area, is the only home of the species of hornbill named after it. Twenty-five years ago there were believed to be about four hundred of these birds in existence, an increase of 100 per cent over the previous fifty years. The Narcondam hornbill has no natural predators and the remoteness and barrenness of the island have kept it largely free of human settlement. Indeed, the hornbill population might have increased still further were it not for the fact that it nests in holes in trees, and mature trees on the island are all too often blown down in the frequent cyclones.

Throughout the islands there are more than 225 species and subspecies of birds, 35 species of mammals, more than 80 species of reptiles and amphibians, at least 20 of which are endemic, and at least 220 species of butterflies. There are also three thousand species of flowering plants, at least five hundred species of non-flowering plants and three hundred species of forest trees. Many of the mammals are introduced, and have thrived in an area of comparatively little human disturbance. The graceful chital or spotted deer, for example, which exists in healthy numbers throughout India, was introduced here only a century ago and has prospered to such an extent that it is considered a pest.

The Andaman/Nicobar chain consists of nearly 306 islands and 260 rocks with a total coastline of 1962 kilometres and a land surface of 8249 square kilometres. The Andaman group (whose name is said to derive from that of the monkey god Hanuman) is by far the larger of the two, having 280 islands covering 6408 square kilometres; the Nicobars have twenty-three islands covering 1841 square kilometres.

The five chief islands, known collectively as the Great Andaman, are separated by narrow straits. The islands themselves consist of a mass of hills enclosing very narrow valleys, all covered in dense tropical forest. The highest point, at 720 metres, is Saddle Peak. The coastline is deeply indented, creating tidal creeks surrounded by mangrove swamps. In more secluded bays are exquisitely coloured coral reefs, which tend to be free of marine vegetation. The inland forests are filled with evergreen trees heavily laden with climbers and creepers, and interspersed with large bamboo glades.

About a hundred kilometres to the east of Great Andaman is Barren Island, the only active volcano in Indian territory, which erupted in 1991 and again in 1995 after lying dormant for two hundred years. As a result, the underwater corals around it are covered in a blanket of black ash.

A mangrove tree at the edge of a beachhead on Havelock Island in the Andamans.

Some 80 per cent of the Nicobar Islands are covered by primary forest, and these areas are vital for endemic bird species: Great Nicobar has 32, Nancowry 36 and Car Nicobar 27. The edible nest swiftlet is one of these species and is much exploited in medicine and Chinese cuisine – it is the principal ingredient of bird's nest soup. Nine million nests a year were exported to China in the early part of this century. The swiftlets make their nests in caves, using echo-sounding to find a suitable location and binding the nest together with their saliva. A survey in 1995 revealed that thirty-six caves were used for this purpose. The enormous demand for nests has severely threatened the future of this remarkable bird, and populations have fallen drastically throughout its range. With an estimated 1100–1800 breeding pairs, the adult swiftlet population in India could be as low as 2500.

In the past these islands were referred to as the Black Waters since it was believed that those who came here never returned. From the early 1800s many attempts were made to settle them, but most of the immigrants died of virulent diseases. The same fate befell a British penal colony established here. Only the local people seemed to be immune to the deadly infections. It was as recently as the 1950s and 1960s that outsiders settled successfully, when the Andaman forests were leased to timber merchants – with interesting repercussions, as we shall see later.

The people who live in the Andaman and Nicobar Islands have long been something of a mystery. Although the census of 1901 revealed a population of 1882 Andamanese and 6511 Nicobarese, there were undoubtedly many indigenous groups completely uncounted. These, however, suffered badly from infection and disease introduced by visitors. Nevertheless, according to the 1981 census, the tribal population had risen to 200,000 divided into six groups: the Andamanese, the Onge, the Sentinalese and the Jarawas in the Andaman Islands, and the Shompens and Nicobarese in the Nicobar Islands. The Andaman tribes, primarily hunter-gatherers, are Negrito and show many similarities to the Semangs of Malaysia and the Aetas of the Philippines. The Nicobarese, mainly horticulturists and herders, are Mongoloid.

The Andamanese speak different dialects of a single language. Because of their isolation, these islanders may be the only 'pure' remnants of the oldest race on Earth. Indeed, the *Imperial Gazetteer of India* (1908) states:

> The antiquity of the Andamanese on their present site is proved by the kitchen-middens [refuse heaps], rising from 12 to 15 feet and more in height, and in some cases having fossilized shells at the base. These show that the Andamanese still get their food just as they did when the now fossil shells contained living organisms.

Early this century the Jarawas were considered the most hostile of the indigenous tribes, alleged to kill strangers on sight with poisonous arrows. Twenty years ago they were still making serious attacks on boats approaching the islands, and some remain very difficult to approach. Intensely animistic, the Andamanese believe in spirits of the sea, the forests and the mountains, but have no form of ceremonial worship. They regard animals, fish and birds as ancestors who have changed shape by supernatural forces.

Coral and red-tailed butterfly fish create an array of startling colours
in the waters of the Andaman Sea.

Unlike the Andamanese, the Nicobarese are territorial rather than tribal, mixing and intermarrying quite easily. They speak six different dialects. Although their religion is also primarily animistic, they believe in spirits and ghosts, performing elaborate ceremonies to exorcize them.

The Nicobarese story of how their people came into being is a strange one. A man and a female dog arrived on a boat from a far-off country and settled in Car Nicobar. In time, the man and dog mated and a son was born. When the son grew up, he killed his father and took his mother as a wife. From these parents the Nicobarese are said to be descended. Even today, in the course of certain rituals, men tie a bow around their forehead, the floppy ends representing the ears of their dog ancestress. The long end of their loincloth represents her tail! Dogs remain important to the Nicobarese and are treated with kindness. Animistic beliefs are also evident in Nicobarese homes, which all contain a *kareau* or spirit-scarer, often in the shape of mythical animals based on fish, crocodiles, birds and pigs.

The Nicobarese never hunt or fish for commercial purposes. Anything surplus to individual requirements is distributed, rather than sold, within the community, a system that appears to work well for those involved. 'Development' has brought many changes to the Andaman and Nicobar Islands, but some of the people hold on to their links with nature and to their ancient beliefs.

Even though they did not manage to settle here, early visitors were struck by the beauty of the islands. In 1874 explorer Allan Hume wrote this lyrical description:

A ridge of rocks or reef on which the surf was breaking lustily, glittering and sparkling in the bright sun, little strips of the whitest possible coral beaches, fringed and bounded by dense mangrove belts composed of trees of many species, those nearest the water low and of the brightest emerald green, those behind more lofty and of a bluer tinge, all backed up by magnificent evergreen forest trees rising tier above tier to the summits of the ridge of low hills.

The water still, as in some little mountain tarn, clear as crystal, here green, there blue of an intensity known only in the tropics, everywhere paved with coral reefs and plateaux, clustered over with marvellously coloured sponges, zoophytes and corallines, and haunted by numerous shoals of still more brilliantly tinted fish, it was like looking down into a garden of another world.

Oriental sweetlips is one of the most striking fish
that frequent the reefs of the Lakshadweep.

Full of miraculously coloured fish, things which I had merely seen in paintings I should have pronounced Turneresque dreams of piscine impossibilities, such shapes, such colours, above all such incredible combination of colours. They were mostly I think what are called rock cods of half a dozen different species – orange, magenta, crimson, blue, green, black, buffy, one bright colour spotted with another...

The whole beach around me moved, while when I moved the beach stood still. The effect was for a few minutes bewildering, but it was soon understood. The whole beach was coated with a layer of dead shells, and every other shell, big and little, contained a hermit crab. These crabs were of all sizes, there were millions and billions of them, they were as the sands of the shores they haunt or the stars in the sky, their numbers were alike incredible and bewildering from the water's edge well into the jungle, and in and about every hole and cranny in all the outermost trees up to heights of at least 20 feet, it was crabs, crabs, crabs.

The Sentinel Islands, in the southern part of the Andaman chain, are home to the world's largest crab, the robber or coconut crab, famed for its ability to climb coconut trees. It points its head upward while climbing and descends head first. Although not as agile as other crabs, its legs, which it arches when walking, support a heavy body: male crabs can weigh 5 kilogrammes. Many naturalists, including Charles Darwin, have reported this crab's ability to break open coconuts by tearing the husk, fibre by fibre. It is said to grip the broken nut with its large left claw and scoop out the coconut flesh with the smaller right claw. While it feeds primarily on coconuts, the robber also eats fish and smaller crabs, and will scavenge on whatever it finds.

On the sand-flats along the coast of the Andamans live swarms of soldier crabs, gregarious creatures which will burrow into the sand at the first sign of danger. Soldier crabs do not scuttle sideways in characteristic crab fashion, but run forwards when the need arises. It is these crabs that are supposed to be the prey of the crab-eating macaques, although this has never been confirmed, and the primates are known also to feed on fruit such as papaya and banana. They can certainly be seen on the beach playing with the crabs, though they flee back to the forest at the sight of a sea snake.

Sea snakes are among the most poisonous snakes in the world, but fortunately their mouths and fangs are too small for them normally to be a threat to humans. They

The robber or coconut crab climbs coconut trees in its effort to feed on the flesh of the coconut.

spend most of their lives at sea, coming on to land only to mate and lay their eggs; though towards the end of the day they can occasionally be seen basking on the sun-baked sand, presumably benefiting from its warmth.

Sea snakes are very vulnerable on land, and even in the water they have to surface every fifteen minutes to breathe. On land or sea, therefore, they frequently fall victim to the swooping attacks of one of the supreme predators of these islands, the white-bellied sea eagle. The eagle grasps the snake in its huge talons and carries it off to its huge nest.

In the twelve-volume journal *Stray Feathers* (1876), edited by the explorer and ornithologist Allan Hume, there is a vivid description of the sea eagle in action:

In the full glare of the noontide sun, his snowy breast shone out with dazzling brightness. The delicate pearly grey of back and wings glistened with an almost silvery sheen. There was an indescribable something in his firm, erect, attitude conveying a sense of majesty and power.

A sea snake glides through the water in search of prey.

*The white-bellied sea eagle is the king of the skies
and is a great predator of sea snakes.*

It is a fine sight to see these eagles, striking one after the other in rapid succession. Soaring far above the highest tree in the island, often I should judge from a height of at least 1000 feet, they come down with nearly closed wings, and with a rushing roar, like that of a cannon ball, in a perfectly direct line, making an angle of 60 degrees with the water which they scarcely seem to reach before they are again mounting with heavy flaps and with a yard or two of snake hanging dead in their talons.

As well as being superb hunters and fishermen, sea eagles are glorious in flight, indulging in fantastic aerial displays. They return to the same nest year after year and defend their territory fiercely, attacking any other eagles that intrude.

One of the most fascinating birds of the Nicobars is the megapode, whose name means large feet. The species found here, *Megapodius freycinet*, was graphically described by C. Boden Kloss, who arrived in 1900 to study the natural history of the islands:

We landed in the afternoon on the eastern shore, and at once set to work cutting a path, for here was the densest kind of Andaman jungle, and although within it one comes across little patches where the bush is fairly open, it is on the whole a wild tangled mass of trunks and branches, bound together by countless ropes of creeping bamboo and thorny rattan.

The forest on shore came right down to the water; and once inside it, we found ourselves in very truth in the home of the megapode. No sooner were we under the trees than we immediately saw the birds, for the jungle is very open, running about singly or in parties of twos and threes. From all round came their cries, perhaps best described as loud, ringing calls, ending in a rapid cackle, to the sound of which the following syllables bear some resemblance, 'urr-rak, urr-rak, ur-r-rak, rak rak, rak, rak!' The megapode hardly ever takes to flight when startled, but runs quickly away among the bushes; the only occasion on which I ever saw these birds use their wings was when once I suddenly walked into a party of four, scratching at the foot of a large tree. Two ran off but the others rose clumsily in the air, and after flying a short distance, attempted to settle on a low branch, on which they alighted very awkwardly, and immediately lost their balance and fell off. The feet, although very large and strong, are not adapted for grasping, and the tail is far too short to be of any use as a balance.

Most megapodes live in lush, wet tropical forests. They all have powerful legs that help in digging their nests, usually on volcanic slopes or around hot-water springs. The nests, which can be anything from 50 centimetres to 2 metres deep, are insulated with volcanic dust, white sand or chips of rocks. Some megapodes have been known to lay their eggs 60 centimetres down on beaches above the high-tide mark. These nest selection habits must have evolved over millions of years, with much trial and error.

The megapode is the only bird not to use its body heat for incubating eggs. In fact, there is no bond at all between parents and young. Several females can lay their eggs in the same mound, and they are incubated by heat generated from the decomposing plants and leaves packed around them. Megapodes gauge the temperature of their nests by dipping their beaks inside and using their tongues, fleshy cheeks or even the solid crest on their heads as thermometers. They then regulate the temperature by adding or removing insulating material as required. This ability to gauge temperature has earned them the nickname of incubator or thermometer birds.

Megapode eggs weigh 250 grammes, five times the weight of a domestic hen's egg. The chicks kick their way out after nearly eighty days and have enough feathers to fly to

A pair of megapodes, the only birds in the world that do not use their body heat for incubating eggs. These birds are restricted to remote islands that are free of predators.

the nearest forest. As there are no large carnivores on the Andaman and Nicobar Islands, the megapode chicks are most vulnerable to predators such as water monitor lizards.

Water monitors, close relatives of the komodo dragons of Indonesia, are the most dramatic-looking inhabitants of the islands. They grow up to 1.8 metres long and not only raid megapode nests for their eggs, but have also been known to lay their own eggs in them – to be tended, cuckoo-style, by the megapodes. Among the mangrove swamps the bold water monitors even raid crocodile nests. As in the Sundarbans of the previous chapter, the mangrove estuarine ecosystem is one of the richest on the islands, providing a habitat for a variety of creatures from tiny mudskippers to large salt-water crocodiles.

Water monitors are widespread, found from Sri Lanka across the Andaman Islands to southern China and as far south as northern Australia. On the mainland and islands of the subcontinent, their preferred habitat is the mangrove swamp. They are extremely adaptable; although they rarely stray far from water, they seem not to mind whether it is fresh or brackish.

The largest of the four species of monitor lizard found on the subcontinent, water monitors are distinguished not only by their size but by the long, narrow head, dark vertical bands on the side of the face, and black body with four or five rows of yellowy white spots across the back. The young are brightly coloured, with more pronounced spots and stripes.

Water monitors are carnivorous, and although they will take carrion they are efficient predators with a fearsome bite; in addition to eggs, their diet includes insects, crabs, fish, birds, rodents, frogs, lizards and snakes, which they capture with a quick rush, shaking their prey vigorously and dashing it against the ground.

Adult monitors spend some months of the year in groups organized under a strict hierarchical system. Just before the mating system, males indulge in a form of ritualistic combat to decide which of them will have the right to mate. Two males stand 'face to face' on their hind legs, clutch each other with their front legs and try to wrestle each other to the ground. This combat is always one-to-one, but may be repeated with different participants over a period of weeks, during which a number of individuals may succeed each other rapidly in the position of dominant male.

I mentioned earlier that in the 1950s the Andaman forests were leased to timber merchants, and this accounts for two small but extraordinary populations of elephants on the islands. Some of the timber companies brought working elephants with them to help with the work, and when one company went bankrupt, forty elephants were abandoned in North Andaman and on Interview Island, where they subsequently went wild in the forests. The Interview Island population of these feral giants now numbers about seventy and a sanctuary has been established to protect them, but their impact on the vegetation of the island has given cause for concern – in a country where so many species are confined to such small areas, anything that upsets the balance can be devastating, and a study has shown that a number of the elephant's favoured food species are declining at an alarming rate.

On Havelock Island, in South Andaman, elephants are still used to drag timber from the forest to the port. At the end of each day's work they are taken down to the sea to cool off. Elephants are naturally strong swimmers, and the company for which they work has trained them to swim up to 3 kilometres across the channel to an adjacent island where the next day's work awaits them. They carry their mahouts on their backs and use their trunks as snorkels. It is quite a sight – elephants in the sea!

Coral paradise

Moving away from these magical islands we watch crowds of terns crashing into the water to feed on the cuttlefish which live in the shallows. Back at the tip of India, at a wonderful place called Kanyakumari, we discover the meeting point of three great expanses of water – the Bay of Bengal, the Arabian Sea and the Indian Ocean. The sea is rough, the waves high and I can still remember the fear I felt when negotiating a small boat through these powerful waters.

To the west of this area lies another cluster of islands, called the Lakshadweep or Hundred Thousand Isles. This is a group of thirty-six coral reefs and islands in the Indian Ocean 220-440 kilometres from the mainland. The islands are small: none exceeds 1.5 kilometres in breadth and the total land area is only about 32 square kilometres. You can walk round some of them in an hour. Most of them run from north to south; across a 150-kilometre channel from the southernmost one lies yet another group of coral islands, the independent republic of the Maldives. Lakshadweep is known to have been inhabited by wandering seafarers since at least the seventh century; at that time Arab traders arrived and the islands were converted to Islam.

The Lakshadweep Islands have to be seen to be believed. A tiny plane lands you on what must be an airstrip in the sea – what a sight as the emerald waters greet you! I was stunned by the fact that even from the plane you could see the bottom of the sea. This sparkling clarity combined itself with the most startling blues and greens that create the carpet of water.

As I boarded a boat and travelled around my gaze was rooted to the water and I watched the corals and enormous leatherback turtles rushing across with the occasional ray in pursuit. It was another world in the water. Finally the temptation sent me on a snorkelling expedition. Mesmerized, I discovered a living realm that will remain etched on my brain forever. It was like watching a kaleidoscope of colours as fish of every hue raced around the corals. Amidst bubbles, gurgles and the intake of much salt water, I went through the experience of a lifetime. Warm water, turquoise lagoons and a sensation that I was enclosed in a vast natural swimming pool with corals, fish, turtles and so much living colour that I sometimes felt I had to rub my eyes in order to believe the vision that lay before me. Scarlet hermit and ghost crabs abound on the beaches, and at night luminescent organisms glow as the tide comes in. It is an idyllic setting as palm trees curl on the edges of the islands and unspoilt white beaches reach for the horizon.

Lakshadweep Islands had transported me back to my childhood, to the time when I read of treasure islands and blue-green seas. Dawn and dusk took on a pink hue as the sun rose and set. The scale of the beauty around me created a desire to discover and explore these treasures of the natural world – real living treasures, in the depth of the waters.

OVERLEAF *Domesticated elephants are now expert swimmers and can even cross a few kilometres in the sea from one island to another in the Andamans.*

The soil of Lakshadweep is light with coral sand beneath, and a metre or so lower is a stratum of coral which stretches right across the islands. Indeed, corals have grown right up to the water's edge and form a barrier between the deep blue open water and the sparkling lagoons. From the air you can see the outer reef margin where the waves crash and form white surf.

To quote another volume of Allan Hume's *Stray Feathers*:

Climbing up the steep sides, the moment we reached the trees, the Ashok, with its innumerable bunches of fiery orange-coloured flowers, attracted the eye. I have often seen this tree in flower elsewhere, but never bearing anything like the same mass of blossom; the whole copse seemed in some places ablaze with it…

Everywhere towering over our heads waved the feather crowns of the finest and tallest coconut trees I have ever seen; the declining sun poured in a perfect flood of golden light through the fretted canopy of softly undulating fronds, imparting to them an almost unearthly brightness. Below, hiding half the pillar-like palm stems, which seemed to stretch away endlessly in all directions, and already shrouded in the gloom of evening, dense masses of breadfruit trees hemmed us around with deep green many-fingered foliage. Lower again infant palms of the most marvellous vigour and symmetry dot the smooth green plots and half conceal the snowy paths.

A land hermit crab on the shores of the Lakshadweep.

*The Lakshadweep are a group of thirty-six coral reefs and islands, sparkling jewels
set in turquoise seas. The colours of the waters change as the sun rises and sets,
creating a vision that is difficult to forget.*

There is plenty of evidence to show how the sea has eroded these islands: sand is washed away, coconut trees are dislodged and fall into the sea. As much as a metre of sand can be washed away each year. This erosion has caused the island of Paralli to be reclaimed by the sea: all that remains is an overturned plinth erected by the Indian government, and it will surely not be long before that, too, disappears from sight.

This constant erosion makes Lakshadweep an unstable environment for both flora and fauna. On many of the islands the hermit crab is the most successful species. As the sun falls, thousands of these crabs emerge from the undergrowth and rush down to the beach in search of food. Being scavengers, they clean the beach very efficiently.

It is in the waters around Lakshadweep that this region's incredible wealth of life is to be found. Here, enchanting coral gardens are created by coral polyps, animals which are close relatives of the sea anemone. But it is only with single-celled algae that coral polyps can produce enormous reef-like structures. For the reef to become a permanent structure and home to other species, the coral blocks must cement together. This happens when the algae die: their plate-like skeletons collapse, filling the tiny cracks and crevices between the corals. Help in cementing the reef also comes from bumphead parrot fish which gather in large shoals near the reef. Their beak-like mouths are specially designed to scrape algae from the rock, and they sometimes bite off chunks of live coral. The digested algae and coral are then excreted as a fine powder which helps hold the reef together.

Coral reefs create curious relationships between otherwise unrelated creatures. More than fifty species of fish and several invertebrates have found a niche in this crowded environment, providing what is best described as a 'cleaning service': they eat scraps of food, mucus and parasites which get lodged in larger fish. The 'cleaners' advertise their services by darting around possible customers and are sometimes even permitted into the mouth to clean the gill chambers.

One of the few predators of these coral reefs is the starfish. It uses its tube feet to climb the coral plate, then opens its stomach to force out digestive juices which enable it to absorb the coral tissues. This process leaves behind a white patch of coral skeleton, but coral can grow back if surrounded by healthy coral tissue.

Coral reefs are also frequented by pennant butterfly fish, powder blue surgeon fish, oriental sweetlips, fusiliers and other species. Shoals of glass fish and the predatory 'tiger grouper' are common sights. The grouper's teeth are simple spikes which give a firm

The crown-of-thorns starfish is a dweller of the coral reef. It absorbs coral tissue by opening its stomach and forcing out digestive juices on to the reef.

Frogfish are difficult to spot since they merge with the algae-covered rocks.

grip on slippery and struggling prey. Fish are therefore swallowed alive and, if spiny, can be a painful meal. Sharp-tailed eels have been found mummified in the bodies of larger spotted groupers.

The grouper has the extraordinary ability to change colour if confronted by an enemy. Its skin is covered by tiny colour cells called chromatophores which can be blinked open or shut. Opening one set and closing another enables colours, spots and stripes to change, causing much confusion in the predator. Large predatory fish of these waters include blue-fin jacks, which can form menacing schools.

The inshore shallows are a fertile union of land and sea, and home to a community of creatures that flourish in the oxygen- and mineral-rich waters. Sturdy seaweeds offer places to hide, while rocks, pebbles and assorted debris provide footholds to which to cling. But this abundance of marine life attracts predators who prowl the shallows looking for easy meals. In order to survive, the marine creatures have evolved some marvellous techniques. Sea anemones contract into leathery lumps when threatened by danger, crabs flatten their bodies into crevices, revealing only their shells, sea urchins anchor their bodies to the rocks, starfish grip stones so powerfully with their suction-cup feet that they will allow their body to be broken rather than relax their grip.

Camouflage is also a vital art in the sea. Fish that are bluish on top but with silvery bellies escape the view of enemies from above as they merge with the water, and from below as they blend with the light in the sky. Mock eyes on the tail of the butterfly fish trick its enemies into attacking its rear, which gives the fish time to dart off. Trumpet fish can form a spire that resembles sponge and hover motionless the instant danger threatens. Frog fish can look remarkably like an algae-covered rock: only their blue eyes betray them. Sargassum fish not only take on the colour of the sargassum weed in which they live, but are also covered with tassels and ribbons which imitate the plant's air-filled flotation bladders. Anemone shrimps are transparent, except for a few visible organs, which again is baffling to potential predators. An anemone has the appearance of a harmless flower, but its tentacles are studded with poison darts that can stun fish.

There is an endless game of hide and seek between predator and prey, and in these crowded seas survival depends on high rates of reproduction. Codfish can lay 5 million eggs in a year and oysters 500 million! One of the best examples of fertility is the diatom, a microscopic plant which reproduces so rapidly that in a single month it may spawn a thousand million descendants!

At about 18 metres the reef slopes away to the sandy seabed. Here, garden eels, which look like sinuous tendrils, anchor themselves by boring a tube into the sand. They can stretch up to 30 centimetres from their tube to snatch food from the water, but quickly retreat if approached by a predator. Here too are sharks, gobies and prawns. These last two have a mutually beneficial relationship: the gobies act as look-outs, warning the virtually blind prawns of danger. In return, the prawns, who share the gobies' burrows, shovel out dirt and thereby uncover food for the gobies to eat.

OVERLEAF *The manta ray, sometimes called the 'devil fish' because of its horns, can make spectacular leaps out of water.*

In the deep waters beyond the reef roam dog-toothed and yellow-fin tuna. The latter are one of the fastest of all swimming fish, their streamlined bodies allowing them to reach speeds of 70 kilometres per hour. They accelerate quickly and can hit top speed in less than a second when they smell food. Impressive though this is, it is not the record; that is held by the sharklike sail fish, which can swim at 110 kilometres per hour – faster than any land animal. Areas frequented by tuna can often be identified by the presence of sooty and noddy terns, seabirds that like to feed on surface molluscs, on which the tuna also prey. The tuna fishermen observing flocks of these birds direct their tiny wooden boats towards them, fishing with the traditional fixed pole and line and swinging the fish out of the water into the boat.

The sea also hides the manta ray. This creature, resembling a giant bat, gets its name from the Spanish for cloak. It has a 'wingspan' of over 5 metres and can weigh more than half a tonne. Its alternative name is the devil fish, because it is black and has a pair of 'horns'. Legends abound about the manta ray 'hugging' swimmers to death or smashing small fishing boats, but they appear to have no basis in fact. It is true that it can make spectacular leaps out of the water, but – despite its nickname and rather fearsome appearance – it is generally a calm creature, cruising through the deep and feeding on shoals of smaller fish.

A variety of sharks and whales also patrol these areas. There are 250 known species of shark in the world, and many of them are found in Indian waters. The whale shark, which reaches nearly 20 metres in length and can weigh 40 tonnes, is the largest fish on Earth. Since sharks are unable to swivel the fins behind their head, they have no 'brakes', so are forced to snatch at prey while on the move. From snout to tail the shark's body is covered with rough scales which can be as deadly as its double rows of needle-sharp teeth.

Their 'skeletons' are made of cartilage and they have a tiny brain, a large part of which is dedicated to the function of smelling. In fact, the shark's sense of smell is so sharp that it can follow a trail just like a sniffer dog and zero in on blood or a dying fish from more than 2 kilometres away. Sharks are great scavengers and will swallow almost anything. They can also store food for many days without digesting it.

Sperm whales, blue whales and humpbacks are all found in the Indian Ocean. Members of the whale family range from 1.35 metres to 34 metres in length and all have a thick layer of blubber to conserve body heat and act as a food reserve in times of scarcity. Large blue whales can weigh 170 tonnes, and their 3.5-metre tails can generate 520 horsepower and speeds of up to 20 knots. Most whales spend much of their time with their mouths open at the bottom of the ocean, swallowing krill and other small creatures. Vast volumes of water filled with potential food flow into their mouths; the

The whale shark is the largest fish on this planet, sometimes reaching 20 metres in length.

enormous tongue is forced backwards from the mouth cavity, allowing this to contract; and the water is forced out again through the baleen (the horny plates that grow from the roof of the mouth). Any food that is too big to pass through this filtering mechanism remains in the massive mouth.

Female blue whales give birth every year and the newborn baby measures 7 metres in length. For seven months it is fed a tonne of rich milk every day while lying on the surface of the sea. By the time it is weaned it is 15 metres long. It will then continue to grow until it reaches the age of twelve years, although it is sexually mature by four or five.

The sperm whale is the only big whale with teeth, which it needs to eat its favourite food, the giant squid. It can dive more than 800 metres to feed and stay below for more than 40 minutes. It gets its name from 'spermaceti', an oily wax found in an extraordinary storage tank in its huge head. This oily wax is believed to aid the whale in deep diving, because it can absorb six times as much nitrogen as blood. Undigested parts of the swallowed squid are sometimes converted into ambergris, an important ingredient in the manufacture of perfume, which in its raw state is a dark sticky material spewed up by the sperm whale and found floating on the water or washed up on beaches.

From above the water, marine biologists can differentiate between species of whales by the different sounds they make. The whistling and clicking sound of the sperm whale contrasts with the low moan of the blue whale, and these ultra-sonic communications can be detected over great distances. When these large whales surface, they exhale a cloud of pressurized steam that can rise vertically for 6 metres. Their exhalations can be heard 1 kilometre away.

Along the west coast

But now back to the western coast of India, into the southern state of Kerala and the backwaters of Cochin, and up the coast to Bombay. Here fishermen depend for their livelihood on a strange fish of the salmon family known as the Bombay duck, widely used for food and sold dried throughout India for use in curries. Some 100,000 tonnes of this one species are taken from the seas every year.

The Bombay duck is translucent and phosphorescent, with a jelly-like body, red jaws and strange backward-curving teeth more suited to a deep-sea monster. In fact, it lives in large shoals in shallow waters and is even sometimes found in the mouths of creeks. Although only 40 centimetres long, it has a voracious appetite and is capable of eating fish larger than itself.

Across a stretch of the Arabian Sea and up towards the Gulf of Kutch, we find a protected area of sea water and coastland, including a chain of forty-two islands, coral reefs, tidal flats and mangroves. The area stretches 200 kilometres from Okha to Jodiya on the Jamnagar coast, and is home to 800 species, including corals, molluscs, crabs, jellyfish, octopuses, sea horses and a wide variety of nesting birds. The 67,000 hectares of sea water and land under protection here has marine life seldom seen elsewhere. Among the 200 species of molluscs are sea hare, conus and octopus; and sea urchins, sea cucumbers and sea slugs are also found here. Large flocks of oystercatchers, snipes, little stints, crab plovers, crested terns, little terns, greater and lesser flamingoes, rosy and spot-billed pelicans, black, white and glossy ibises and herons are part of the rich bird life of the area.

The most unusual part of this coastline is the Gulf of Kutch itself, where the sea meets the desert. Here on the mud-flats is a major nesting colony of greater flamingoes; in some years as many as 20,000 nests are occupied. The nests are made of soft mud, left behind when the monsoon waters recede and smoothly plastered into a mound. Some are built on old nest sites, but others are brand new. The biggest can be 60 centimetres high and 40 centimetres across, and may be separated from their neighbours by as little as 30 centimetres. As the flamingoes paddle in the mud, they use their beaks to build a mudbank that will protect the nests from any increase in water level. A crater-like depression on top of the mound helps drain off any excess water. The mounds are as hard as metal because of the high salt content in the mud.

Chicks are fed on regurgitated food – blue-green algae, crustaceans and other microbes – for more than a week, after which they live as part of the larger commune. Shivrajkumar of Jasdan, R. M. Naik and K. S. Lavkumar wrote movingly about this colony in *The Journal of the Bombay Natural History Society* (1960):

> The sight of the flamingoes was beyond belief. The fabulous birds were atop their mound-like nests, some standing, others sitting, their graceful necks curved over their heads. Every now and then, heads would rise high and pink wings would open and flash in display and the soft murmuring from the tending birds rose incessantly like distant surf on rocks.
>
> A sight indeed worthy of the gods! There we sat in the blazing sun with the amazing spectacle spread before us. Years of longing had at last come true and in a dreamlike comprehension, we scanned the great expanses of baked mud, the clustered mounds of mud nests rising from them and the graceful pink forms poised above.

From the flamingo colony it is a long voyage through shallow, muddy sea water to our next destinations – the Great Rann of Kutch, the Little Rann of Kutch and the Thar Desert of Rajasthan. When we reach dry land the journey will continue on camels over rough and slippery ground. It will be a journey to remember.

OVERLEAF *Flamingoes feast where the desert meets the sea. Monsoon winds have blown the sea inland with a rich cocktail of sea food.*

CHAPTER FOUR

HARSH DESERTS

I AM STANDING AT THE EDGE of the Little Rann of Kutch, in the state of Gujarat, northwestern India. Far away on the horizon is the Gulf of Kutch, whose waters sweep nearly 80 kilometres through a creek to meet the salt-flats of the Little Rann. Strong winds from the southwest blow sea water in on one side, while rivers empty into it on the other. During the monsoon, when salt and fresh water combine, this barren wasteland turns into a sheet of water some 30–210 centimetres deep.

Two months later, when the waters begin to recede, the flats quickly dry out, becoming cracked and desert-like. Salt crystals glitter in the sun like a sea of glass and create bizarre reflections and mirages: wild asses look like prehistoric giraffes, trees turn into giants, lakes appear and disappear.

Early travellers to this salt-impregnated wilderness called it 'a space without a counterpart in the globe'. One of them, James Todd, described it in *Annals and Antiquities of Rajasthan* (1920):

> This immense salt-marsh, upwards of one hundred and fifty miles in breadth, is formed chiefly by the Luni, which, like the Rhône, after forming Lake Leman, resumes its name at its further outlet, and ends as it commences with a sacred character, having the temple of Narayan at its embouchure, where it mingles with the ocean, and that of Brahma at its source of Pushkar. The Rann, or Ran, is a corruption of Aranya, or 'the waste', nor can anything in nature be more dreary in the dry weather than this parched desert of salt and mud, the peculiar abode of the khar-gadha, or wild-ass, whose love of solitude has been commemorated by an immortal pen. That this enormous depository of salt is of no recent formation we are informed by the Greek writers, whose notice it did not escape... Although mainly indebted to the Luni for its salt, whose bed and that of its

The elegant chinkara or Indian gazelle can survive on the moisture
contained within the vegetation of the desert.

165

feeders are covered with saline deposits, it is also supplied by the overflowings of the Indus, to which grand stream it may be indebted for its volume of water.

The Rann lies along a line of marine recession between the Indus delta and the Gulf of Khambhat, which formed through geological processes in the Pleistocene age. Geologists are certain that the present Rann of Kutch was once part of the sea, and it is known that in 325 BC the area was a navigable lake. It is only as a result of frequent earthquakes in the first half of the nineteenth century that the Rann rose to its present level. Its shallow bed was subsequently filled with silt and clay, which are discharged into it by a number of rivers. The porous nature of its upper soil – a mixture of stone, shingle and salt – makes storing water in ponds and reservoirs difficult, but brackish water is found in rocks close to the surface.

The floodwaters are a nursery for millions of shrimps and other marine life, and as they recede, vast flocks of flamingoes arrive to feast. Their approach is an extraordinary sight: the sky is almost obliterated by shades of pink and magenta. Soon the water is jammed with over half a million flamingoes gorging themselves on the shrimp population. Alongside these colourful birds are scores of fishing boats, their occupants also keen to harvest the glut of seafood. On the shore refrigerated trucks wait to rush the catch to the urban centres of India. In another ten days the 'harvest' will be over and an army of salt workers will arrive to collect 25 per cent of India's annual supply. Finally, the cracked earth is left carpeted with a thin film of fertile dust, which is blown across the Rann into agricultural fields – a welcome bonus to local farmers.

Wildlife of the Little Rann

Around 100 years ago the edges of the salt-flats were frequented by leopards, cheetahs and even lions. Today they are the preserve of the Indian wild ass, the large carnivores having become extinct in this area.

There are five species of Asiatic wild ass, including the Tibetan one we met in Chapter 1, and their total population does not exceed 25,000. The Indian wild ass found in the Rann of Kutch, which is distinguished by its dark brown coat, numbers a mere 2000.

Wild asses graze widely, migrating long distances, and are perfectly adapted to the monsoon floods. In fact, local people follow their footsteps when negotiating the mud-flats and quicksand. At the height of the rains the asses take refuge on small dirt mounds called bets which are scattered across the area.

The monsoon is the most exciting time to observe the Indian wild ass: this is when

foaling, courtship and mating occur. Gestation lasts ten to eleven months, and a few weeks after foaling females come into heat again. They gather in large groups to protect their young, but the groups gradually disperse as the foals become strong enough to walk long distances. Grooming each other's neck is a frequent social activity, and they also enjoy rolling in the dust that cakes the mud-flats.

Much of the wild ass's daily life is determined by range and territory. Dominant stallions each have their own territory, across which females and young may wander. By smelling urine and droppings a stallion determines which of the mares has come into oestrus and then commences his courtship. Any other stallions who try to encroach are chased away with much angry kicking, snorting and shaking of the head. The female usually rebuffs the stallion's first attempts at mating by kicking out at him, but she soon becomes receptive. During this period a stallion will mate with several mares and aggressively prevent any of them from leaving his territory.

In one herd of wild ass that we watched, a real-life drama was unfolding. The dominant male, known as Mr Mondale, had been in control of a harem of twenty-six females for twelve years and had doubtless fought off many challenges to his supremacy. However,

The Indian wild ass is found only in the Rann of Kutch and is endemic to the area. Dominant males have been known to control a harem of more than twenty-six females for over twelve years.

Mr Mondale was past his prime – in 1995 he had sired only eight foals, not enough to ensure the healthy survival of the herd. It was only a matter of time before one of his own sons deposed him and forced him out of the territory.

Mr Mondale's predecessor was still around, a battered old male with chewed ears and half a tail; he was known as the Rapist because of his habit of sneaking back into the herd in an attempt to liaise with one of the females. When Mr Mondale is no longer top male, he will join the Rapist here on the fringes of wild ass society.

The Wild Ass sanctuary of Dhrangadhra was established in the Little Rann in 1973 specifically to protect the Indian wild ass. However, the whole habitat is threatened by salt exploitation, shrimp farming, agricultural encroachment and the grazing of millions of livestock. These pressures have forced the wild ass into agricultural fields, but so far the local farmers seem to be exhibiting remarkable tolerance towards it. The wild ass's future may not, therefore, be completely bleak.

A small population of the Indian wolf also stalks this saline desert in search of prey. In the past large packs haunted the *vidis*, or traditional grasslands, but this habitat has all but disappeared and the wolves now survive by the skin of their teeth. Among the small packs remaining, only the dominant female gives birth; she and her mate are referred to as the 'alpha' pair. They assert their power in the pack's hierarchy by deciding where to hunt and shelter. They also feed first on any kill.

The whole pack assists in rearing the pups. A secluded spot is selected as a den and may sometimes be used again and again over a period of several years. An average litter consists of five pups, but can number as many as twelve. Small pups are left in the den or hidden in bushes when the adults go off hunting. For the first six months, until the pups are able to join in the hunting excursions, both parents carry kills back to the den or regurgitate food to feed the young.

Adult wolves are territorial and mark their area by urinating and rubbing their scent on bushes and shrubs. Sound also plays an important part in their social behaviour; their howls resound over large distances, warning any intruders of their presence. Eating habits depend on the availability of food but, thanks to a distensible stomach, they can eat five times their normal weight at one sitting. Like other predators, they need to gorge themselves whenever the opportunity arises, as they cannot predict when their next successful hunt will be.

OVERLEAF *The black buck is an antelope sacred for many desert people in India; most black buck populations survive only because of the protection afforded to them by local communities.*

One of the wolf's favourite prey species is the black buck, the region's sole surviving antelope. Until a few decades ago millions of black buck roamed the subcontinent, but poaching and loss of habitat have rendered it extinct in Bangladesh and Pakistan, and reduced its population to a mere handful in Nepal. Nowadays, there are an estimated 40,000 black buck in India, and its declining numbers have in turn affected wolf populations.

Tiny groups of black buck survive on the edges of the salt-flats, and larger populations are found near villages and agricultural fields where local people protect and worship them. The inhabitants of several villages around the Little and Great Ranns believe that the black buck is a harbinger of the monsoon and a symbol of fertility, so it is tolerated irrespective of the damage it inflicts on crops. Some villagers believe that black buck feed only on grasses, sedges and other weeds in the crop fields, thereby doing a service to the farmer.

The connection between man and black buck goes back thousands of years. According to Hindu mythology, the black buck is a sacred animal, so its skin is sanctified and used as a seat in religious ceremonies: Indian *sadhus*, saints and hermits are commonly seen seated on black buck or chital skin. Even a glimpse of this antelope is considered auspicious. The black buck has frequently been depicted in paintings and sculptures, most famously, perhaps, on the western pillar of the southern gate of Sanchi, the great Buddhist relic mound near the city of Bhopal in central India. The poet Kalidasa's epic drama *Shakuntala*, written in the third century, mentions tame black bucks living in the *ashram* (religious retreat) of the saint Kanava Rishi. The animal was always found in the company of those absorbed in deep meditation or religious learning.

Adult male black bucks usually measure 70–80 centimetres at the shoulder and can weigh more than 40 kilogrammes. Their horns can be 50 centimetres long or more. Females do not have horns and are much smaller and daintier. Both sexes have an impressive turn of speed and can reach 110 kilometres per hour, an ability they probably developed in order to help them escape from the even faster (but now extinct) cheetah.

Black buck are not always black. Indeed, only mature males in the breeding season really deserve the name; at other times they are a sort of sandy grey-brown, as are females and juveniles throughout the year. The males' darkening colour is caused by increasing amounts of the hormone testosterone in their bloodstream as the time for mating approaches. Dominant males turn black first and courtship commences amid much sparring. The males strut around, proudly defending their territories and pursuing receptive females with flamboyant courtship displays. Clashes between males are sometimes vicious, continuing until one submits. Females can give birth twice a year, on each occasion to a single fawn. Within days the young are leaping and springing into the air, exercising their limbs with abandon.

An old and vigilant female is in charge of the herd, relying on her sharp eyesight to detect danger. At the slightest suspicion of alarm, mother and young bound away. Black buck start grazing at first light to take advantage of the early morning dew. This ensures that they are not dependent on water-holes and can therefore survive droughts by foraging on moisture-laden vegetation.

The lion's last refuge

Also on the fringes of the desert lies the Gir forest at the southern tip of the Kathiawar peninsula, a protected area of 1500 square kilometres of grassland and forest where the Asiatic lion has lived in harmony with local people for centuries, walking through villages at all times of day. Some groups have settled near the coastline, where there is little forest. They have even been seen on the beaches, having travelled 40 kilometres from their forest homes: a group of twenty-one was counted there on one occasion in 1996.

There are hardly any recorded cases of man-eating lions, and few of poaching and poisoning. Indeed, considering that lions kill and eat hundreds of livestock every year, there seems to be a surprising degree of peace and tolerance between man and animal. My diary notes reflect this:

It is 7 a.m. and the sun peeps over the horizon. I am bumping along in an old jeep through the forests of Gir when suddenly the wireless crackles. Three lionesses and six cubs have been seen by a milkman a few kilometres down the road. We rush off to investigate. The forest looks lush and green now the monsoon rains are over. The grass is high and visibility low. In a few months' time this deciduous habitat will have burnt up under a scorching sun.

After a short distance several men wave at us and we come to a grinding halt. Some of them are whistling and making strange grunting noises like those made by cow-herders. I am surprised at the noise but am informed that this is how people in Gir interact with the lion. I soon join my companions on foot in a dash through the forest and high grass. Everybody is trying to spot the lions and our noise is greeted by low roars from a lion we are unable to see. I object to our causing this disturbance, knowing that under similar circumstances tigers would simply vanish, and insist on returning to the jeep. We slowly drive about

100 metres further on, only to find two cubs darting across the road watched from the edge of the grass by a lioness. My companions continue to make strange noises and the lioness watches us curiously. Soon the pride moves off. It is my very first glimpse of the Asiatic lion.

On a more recent visit to the area I was stunned to find how tolerant these lions were of human observers. From a distance of 8 metres I stood and watched a pair of mating lions as they entangled themselves in one another amid an orchestra of roars and groans. Over a period of two days the lioness seduced the lion over and over again; they remained around the shade of a dry river bed mating a few times every hour.

On the same trip, and again from only a few metres away, I watched a lioness suckling her three young cubs. Amid much licking and cuddling the cubs jumped over their mother. At one point the scene was interrupted by a lone hyena who walked by, 50 metres away. When the lioness saw it she bounded towards it but the hyena scampered off. Mother and cubs went back to their cuddling and suckling as the early morning sun glanced off their coats. The lioness started to lick one of the cubs thoroughly. Another squeezed in to nuzzle her face and the third watched me curiously. Suddenly the mother flopped down on her side and the cubs began to suckle again. I left them, but the scene will remain with me forever.

The low-lying hills of Gir are volcanic in origin and the entire forest is surrounded by agricultural fields. The monsoon brings little rain here, so the five perennial rivers and countless streams that criss-cross the forest are a vital source of water. The forest itself is made up mostly of stunted teak and open savannah grassland, interspersed with patches of thorny deciduous forest. A few evergreen riverine tracts line the permanent water-courses. Leopards share this habitat with the lions, and also share their liking for deer and domestic livestock. This makes the forest of Gir one of the finest places to observe these two large cats.

The Asiatic lion is believed once to have ranged across Syria, Iraq, Iran, Pakistan and most of northern and central India. At one time there were thousands of them spread across the northwest corner of India. However, rampant hunting and large-scale agricultural conversion of forest land forced them into virtual extinction by the end of the nineteenth century. In 1880 there seem to have been only twelve lions in Gir; by

*The Asiatic lion is now restricted to the Kathiawar peninsula in western India.
It is very tolerant of human presence and seldom attacks man.*

1920 this figure had risen to 50, by 1936 to 287, and the present number is said to be over 300. However, despite these encouraging figures, the Asiatic lion's future cannot be considered secure: what biologists call lack of genetic diversity – inbreeding – poses a threat to a small population of any animal, and the fact that there is only one surviving population means that a single disaster such as disease or destruction of the habitat could wipe out the entire species.

Asiatic lions can be distinguished from African lions by a fairly prominent fold of skin on their abdomen or belly. The other obvious difference is that the Asiatic lion lacks the African species' luxuriant mane.

Lions live in permanent social groups (prides) consisting of related adult females and their young in one group. Males are evicted from their natal pride when they reach maturity and have to establish their own territory and find another pride of lionesses with which to mate. In order to do this they must evict the resident males, and these conflicts can be bloody. A single male lion is unlikely to be successful in taking over a pride; most prides have two or three resident males, often brothers or cousins who left their own pride together, though sometimes unrelated males who teamed up during the period they spent as territory-less nomads. Lionesses can reproduce from the age of three. Adult males seldom acquire a home range before the age of five, but then they mark their territories and vocalize regularly, unlike females, who rarely roar. A male's territory can encompass 150–200 square kilometres, but the females' territory is much smaller – around 60–80 square kilometres. Seasonal fluctuations in home ranges occur, especially between the dry and wet season. Females do most of the hunting, traditionally as a team; their combined strength enables them to bring down much larger prey than they could hope to kill on their own. However, in the dense forest at the centre of the Gir National Park it has been observed that lions frequently hunt alone – perhaps because the dense vegetation makes visual contact with others of the pride more difficult.

The Great Indian Desert

The Rann of Kutch is only a small part of the great desert area that straddles the border between India and Pakistan. The Great Indian Desert, or Thar Desert, covers some 446,000 square kilometres and ranges over six states – Punjab and Sind in Pakistan, and the Punjab, Haryana, Rajasthan and Gujarat in India. In contrast to the saline desert of the Rann, this is a predominantly sandy area interspersed with hillocks and gravel plains. Louis Rousselet, writing in 1892, described the desert of Rajasthan like this:

*An Asiatic lion at edge of the sea. Small prides have moved
to colonize new areas on the coastline.*

The desert of the Sahara does not present a more desolate appearance than did
the scene before us. A few stunted bushes, and here and there a blackened rock,
appeared above the waves of shifting sand, which was ploughed into long
furrows by the wind; and this dismal landscape was enlivened by a herd of
gazelles drinking at a clear pool of water, which, taking to flight at our
approach, disappeared among the sandy ravines. The first rays of the rising sun
suddenly lit up the rugged mountain-tops, and for a few minutes the scene was
grand; but the light soon overspread the whole landscape, which once more
became tame and desolate. On leaving the mountains we came upon a vast and
arid plain, extending to a long line of blue mountains, beyond which lies
Kishengurh. I shall never forget the interminable march across this desert. The
sun pouring down on the bare ground rendered the atmosphere stifling, while a
hot wind raised from time to time a cloud of fine dust which parched our
throats and brought the tears into our eyes.

James Todd, a few years earlier, compared the desert to a tiger:

> Instead of the ancient Roman simile, which likened Africa to the leopard's hide, reckoning the spots thereon as the oases, I would compare the Indian desert to that of the tiger, of which the long dark stripes would indicate the expansive belts of sand, elevated upon a plain only less sandy, and over whose surface numerous thinly peopled towns and hamlets are scattered.

In these barren wastelands the vegetation is unique. The fact that plants are able to grow in temperatures of over 50°C is startling in itself, and the sand dunes of these western deserts, where temperatures reach 54°C, house a remarkably rich natural world. Many plants have lengthy root systems that probe deep down into the soil to find water. Desert cacti have more spines than leaves, thus minimizing evaporation. They store water from occasional torrential downpours in their stems for use in hotter and drier times. Desert flowers, of which there are a surprising number, have tiny leaves, also to minimize water loss. Alongside these plants grow the adaptable acacia and khejri (*Prosopis cineraria*) trees.

The Flora of the Indian Desert by E. Blatter and Professor F. Hallberg, published by the Bombay Natural History Society in 1917, provided this summary:

> It is clear that the climate is hostile to all vegetation, only plants possessing special adaptations being able to establish themselves. These adaptations are in general of two types, having two distinct objects in view: to enable the plant to obtain water, and to retain it when obtained.
>
> The bulk of the vegetation consists of a kind of scrub made up of shrubs and perennial herbs, capable of great drought resistance and of a period of comparative rest, extending throughout the greater part of the year. There are few trees to be seen, and these are stunted and generally thorny or prickly, thus protecting themselves against plant-feeding animals. Of the latter, there are vast herds of camels, cattle, sheep and goats, forming the chief wealth of the rural population, and appearing to thrive in spite of the arid nature of the country…
>
> The action of the wind on the sand results in the formation of dunes of various shapes, depending on the local configuration of the country, on the variation in strength and direction of the wind, and on the supply of material. Sometimes they form with extreme rapidity, a railway track being covered in a few hours.

The desert peoples

Hot and parched though it is, the Thar Desert is the most populous desert in the world, with some 84 people per square kilometre. (In the Sahara there are 0.4 people per square kilometre, and in the Namib even fewer.) Life centres around the water-holes, where turtles and fish feed on the scraps left by women who come there to wash their cooking pots.

Perhaps the most remarkable of the desert people are the Bishnoi, members of a sect which believes in complete non-violence to all living organisms; they are the primary reason that desert wildlife still exists on the subcontinent. The women of the community have been known to breast-feed black buck fawns and save insect life, while many of the men have died in their efforts to counter armed poaching gangs. Bishnoi, founded in 1542, is an offshoot of Jainism, which teaches that all nature's creations have a right to life. This belief reached its apotheosis in 1778 when 294 men and 69 women laid down their lives to protect the khejri tree. A senior officer of Jodhpur state arrived to cut down the trees, which were needed for burning lime. The first to challenge him was a woman, who hugged one of the trees and was promptly decapitated. Her three daughters followed suit and were also axed. Many others followed them, until 363 Bishnoi lay dead. This mass slaughter led to a royal order that prohibited the cutting of any tree in a Bishnoi village. A temple was later constructed at Khejarli in memory of the 363 dead, and every year thousands of Bishnoi arrive to commemorate the sacrifice of their ancestors.

I went on a pilgrimage to this spot at the edge of the desert. Amid a grove of shady trees I realized that two hundred years ago the earth on which I was standing must have been drenched in blood. As I looked around, a couple of peacocks and a chinkara (Indian gazelle) passed by. In the temple I was reminded that the Bishnoi bury chinkara that die and even erect stones to mark their graves.

But it is the khejri tree that is particularly special to the Bishnoi: its leaves are essential fodder for livestock, its thorns help to protect the desert dwellers from wild animals, its pods are a vital foodstuff and its branches are lopped for firewood.

It is remarkable how desert wildlife thrives around Bishnoi settlements. A network of natural sanctuaries has resulted from beliefs rooted in the past and will ensure the survival of many species in the future.

OVERLEAF *The Bishnoi are a community that believes in the protection of anything that lives – plant or animal. Over the centuries hundreds have lost their lives in order that a tree or an antelope can survive.*

People throughout the desert use camels as beasts of burden. The camel's ability to go without water for ten days in the hottest conditions and up to twenty in the cooler weather makes it a valued possession.

Anyone wishing to buy or sell a camel converges in November on the little village of Pushkar, on the edge of the Thar Desert; here, for a few days around the time of the full moon, the most sacred lake in India, said to have formed on the spot where a lotus flower fell from the hand of Brahma, attracts some 300,000 pilgrims from all over Rajasthan. Although this is primarily a time of worship, when pilgrims bathe in the holy waters and pray for prosperity in the year to come, it is also the occasion of an enormous livestock fair, when thousands of camels, cattle and horses change hands. Camels offered for sale are carefully groomed: tics are removed from their long hair, all traces of dirt washed off and their coats are brushed and polished. They are then bedecked with brightly coloured dyes, jewellery and cloths of cotton or silk.

Only male camels are used for work, although the females are important sources of milk and butter. Camels seem to become attached to their human handlers, but during the mating season males can be very aggressive towards each other, bellowing, charging, crashing their necks together and spraying in all directions, beating their tails back and forth as they urinate. Strangely, they then seem to have great difficulty mating and may have to be assisted by their owners.

Adapting to life in the desert

Desert life in all its forms has evolved to tolerate the intense heat, whether it be the camel's nasal membrane, which prevents water vapour from escaping, or the use of underground burrows to keep cool, or the long legs of the gazelle that keep its body well clear of the scorching ground. Most desert animals can tolerate high levels of salinity, secreting excess salts through special glands. Saline depressions fill up during the monsoon, then dry out, leaving behind concentrated brine. Grasses and sedges grow around the edges of these depressions, providing a vital food source for grazing animals. Some fish are equipped with a lung so that when pools become too brackish or dry out completely, they can change over to breathing air, flapping around in the mud as they wait for the rains to come again. Others, like the so-called annual fish, die when there is no longer enough water to support them, having first laid very tough eggs which can survive in the mud until next year's rains. Turtles burrow deep into the mud, entering a state of suspended animation until the life-giving monsoon comes again.

Other creatures cope with the intense heat by becoming nocturnal. One of the most intriguing of these is the ratel or honey badger, a small, solidly built and very fierce creature with short legs and a stumpy tail. It has a wide-ranging diet, from honey and fruit to mammals, birds, reptiles and carrion.

I will never forget my own experiences of the desert. On one occasion I spent a very special day surrounded by sun, sand and moon near the tiny village of Chordia, deep in the Great Indian Desert. I explored stretches of sand dunes interspersed with scrub land. The sun was lifting over the horizon, splashing across the patterns of the dunes. A few black beetles scampered across the sand, while over a nearby rise a desert fox appeared. I crouched down and watched as it walked on the ridge, pausing for a moment to eat a beetle. Further down a group of six chinkara had left the safety of the scrub and were walking up a dune. The fox watched them alertly but found no young to prey on. It moved on, observed carefully by the chinkara. A gerbil scampered across the scrub and a harrier swooped down without success.

Away in the distance I saw the thatched roofs of a tiny village. Steeped in folklore and stories of courage, love, devotion and sacrifice, this is the land of the Rajput warriors, of maharajahs and princes. A woman in a bright red *ghagra* (skirt) crossed the edge of a sand dune, reminding me that human culture has fought the harshness of the desert with colour, music, song, dance and ingenuity. But human ingenuity is no match for the ingenuity of nature.

My approach startled a group of about thirty chinkara, who ran towards the ridge of the dunes. I watched as the sun slipped over the horizon and the full moon appeared. The two orbs faced each other for a second and time seemed to stand still. As night fell, the moonlight created a landscape so surreal that I had to remind myself that this was not a dream or an illusion. Desert nights are spectacular, and near a village the nocturnal sounds of animals can give way to an assortment of music from the *morchung*, the *srangi*, the *nar* and the *algooja* – musical instruments whose haunting sounds convey something of the uniqueness of the desert.

The chinkara is one of the most adaptable of the desert animals. It thrives in and around sand dunes, undulating slopes and fallow lands. Like the black buck, it prefers moisture-laden flowers and leaves, and can metabolize sufficient water from these to survive without depending on water-holes. It also avoids dehydration by resting in the shade during the middle of the day.

Both male and female chinkaras have ringed horns, and tufts of hair growing from their knees. They stand 65 centimetres at the shoulder and a fully grown animal can

OVERLEAF *The Thar Desert. Harsh and inhospitable, this region is home to a diversity of flora and fauna that have adjusted to the lack of water.*

weigh more than 20 kilogrammes. They live in small groups of five to fifteen, and the males are very territorial. Clashes between males are aggressive and the victor rushes towards the female to commence his courtship and mating. Newborn fawns are tiny and keep close to their mothers in the first months of life.

When alarmed, a chinkara races off but stops suddenly after about 200 metres, looking around for the source of possible danger. Small populations of chinkara abound in Ranthambhore National Park at the edge of the desert, and I have occasionally watched a tiger stalking mother and young, but each time the chinkara's alertness, a shrill whistling alarm call and a few bounds saved them from the tiger's pounce.

Desert predators

The desert cat, or Asiatic wild cat, loves scrubland and is most common in the Thar Desert in Rajasthan. It is slightly larger than a domestic cat, weighing 3–4 kilogrammes, and its yellow brown fur and black spots provide excellent camouflage in the sand. It is nocturnal, spending its days in burrows dug into the sand, and as a result not a great deal is known of its habits. It feeds on jerboa, gerbils, voles and mice, with occasional hares, birds, insects, lizards and even snakes. Mating probably occurs throughout the year but is at its peak in March-April and November-December, with cubs born two months later. During the cubs' first few months of life the mother brings them injured prey in order to teach them the techniques of hunting. She is a solo parent; the male appears to play no part in the rearing of the cubs.

A slightly larger cat that thrives in arid areas and frequents the edges of the desert is the caracal, one of the most beautiful of felines. Slim and graceful, it has a sleek coat that varies from fawn to grey in colour, but may be a gloriously rich reddish brown. Its pointed ears are tufted with black or grey hair, and it has a short tail like its close relative the lynx.

Like the cheetah, the caracal was once trained to hunt on behalf of kings, emperors and the nobility. It is also known as the gazelle cat because of its reported ability to kill gazelles. Only tiny populations survive on the Indian subcontinent and little is known about its habits. However, I have watched caracals in the dry forests of Ranthambhore, and have seen the close relationship between mother and cubs and their ability to evade danger especially from tigers and leopards.

Rare and elusive, the caracal is seldom seen. Like the cheetah
it was trained over the centuries to hunt for kings and emperors.
Today it is extinct in most of its former range.

Another predator of the desert is the desert fox, which is grey with long ears, a bushy tail and long hairs on the pads of its feet to provide insulation against the hot desert sand. It constructs its burrow near colonies of gerbils, thus ensuring a ready and convenient source of food. It is active in the cooler hours of the day and thereby avoids water loss by evaporation. Much of its water intake comes from the prey it eats. During the summer desert foxes eat 'ber' fruit, water melons and seeds, but their diet consists chiefly of rodents, hares, birds, reptiles and the occasional scorpion. A favourite prey species is the sanda or spiny-tailed lizard. Pups are born blind and remain in the burrow for five weeks, during which time their parents feed them regurgitated food.

Gerbils are one of the many desert creatures who appear to need no water at all. Among the ruins of a desert town some 50 kilometres from the nearest water source, a colony of gerbils sustains a thriving wildlife community: snakes and birds of prey such as harriers and short-toed eagles use these little rodents as a source of both food and water. Gerbils' hearing is so sensitive that they can tell by the sound of wing-beats whether or not an approaching bird is a threat. They thump the ground to warn others of impending danger.

Desert reptiles

Reptiles thrive in desert regions and the sanda, which grows to about 30 centimetres in length, is a typical resident of the Thar. Each of a series of burrows made on hard, flat earth with openings at the surface accommodates one individual and provides it with enough space to turn round. Sandas emerge after sunrise, but at the slightest hint of danger they rush back into their burrows, sometimes choosing the wrong one if they are in a desperate hurry! At night the burrow opening is sealed by a soil 'plug' which prevents the entry of predators, such as desert foxes, monitor lizards and even tawny eagles. Sandas lay clutches of 8–15 eggs at the opening of their burrows, and the young are taken inside as soon as they hatch. The body fat of sandas is supposed to possess aphrodisiac properties, making it vulnerable to human predators.

Many species of snake abound in the desert. Snakes are sensitive to vibrations on the ground, but their hearing is poor. Their sense of smell, however, is well developed, and they use their tongues to pick up scents from air and earth. This is how they locate mates, smell predators and track their prey. As cold-blooded animals, they respond to the temperature around them and become more or less active accordingly.

The apparent sluggishness of some snakes in hot weather can be deceptive, however. The Russell's viper is a heavy-bodied snake, yellowish brown in colour, with a triangular head and distinctive chain-like pattern on its back. Predominantly nocturnal, it may

The desert fox is active only after the sun sets. The long hair on the pads of its feet provides protection from these burning sands so that it can stalk and hunt.

seem to be asleep during the heat of the day, but if disturbed it will respond fiercely. A loud hissing sound should warn the intruder that the snake is annoyed, but if this is not heeded the Russell's may strike with alarming speed and its bite is frequently fatal. It is particularly dangerous in the desert, where its colours blend almost perfectly with the sand.

Even more lethal than the Russell's is the saw-scaled viper, which injects enough venom to kill between seven and twelve men with one bite. Yet in comparison with

OVERLEAF *The spiny-tailed lizard or sanda is a typical inhabitant of the desert. It has been ruthlessly slaughtered for its body fat which is said to possess aphrodisiac properties.*

The saw-scaled viper is only 30 centimetres long, but its venom is deadly.

the Russell's and the cobra this is a tiny snake – only about 30 centimetres long, though one giant captured in the Thar Desert measured 81 centimetres. It gets its name from the serrated scales which it can rub together to make the threatening sound which serves as its defence mechanism. It lives crouched up in small depressions and pits, giving a series of warning hisses if any intruders approach.

Unlike many snakes, the saw-scaled viper does not leave a recognizable serpentine track in its wake. Instead it moves in a sideways looping motion, often lifting itself right off the ground to speed its progress. The result is an S-shaped trail that makes it impossible for inexpert observers to tell which way it is going.

Bird life in the desert

The most delicate and exquisitely coloured bird that frequents the desert areas is the sand grouse. In the early morning thousands of these speckled brown birds gather at water-holes to quench their thirst, making an astonishing amount of noise in the process. Then suddenly they vanish and silence descends until another day.

The painted sand grouse is also astounding in its beauty; the male has white and
black on the forehead and a chestnut, fawn and black breast band. Painted sand grouse
nest on hard, flat ground, their colours blending so perfectly into the desert that, even
from a metre or so away, they can barely be seen. The young are able to forage seeds for
themselves, but cannot reach water. To solve this problem the adult male flies to the
nearest water-hole and soaks his absorbent breast feathers. He then returns to the
chicks and allows them to drink from his saturated body.

*A flock of Indian sand grouse, a desert bird which has adapted to the harsh climate. It can collect
water in its breast feathers and carry it to the chicks hidden some distance away.*

The desert communities have unique links with migratory birds. In the small village of Kheechan, right in the centre of the Thar Desert, the people feed thousands of demoiselle cranes between September and March. The demoiselle is the smallest of the five crane species found in India and is dark grey with white ear tufts behind its bright crimson eyes. It is a winter visitor to the desert, its breeding grounds stretching from southeast Europe to Mongolia.

In Kheechan, a *chugga ghar*, or feeding home, stores the grain used to feed the cranes. The high-pitched calls of the birds at first light are the signal for one of the village men to scatter grain all over the area. Soon the sky darkens as thousands of cranes arrive to feast, often less than 5 metres from the village folk with whom they have established a bond of trust over decades. The kindness of the villagers has a high price, however, as it costs several thousand pounds a year to provide the hundred tonnes of grain required to feed the birds: a staggering sum if you consider that the average per capita income in this community is less than forty pounds a year.

The cranes' daily routine is to feed at sunrise, then gather a few hundred metres away on sand dunes to groom their delicate feathers. Flying formations are usually led by a female, and soon after grooming the birds fly off to adjacent agricultural fields to round off their meal with seeds and lime-rich soil crumbs. They are constantly alert; unexpected intrusions result in alarm calls and thousands of birds rapidly taking off into the sky. As the sun rises higher, the cranes quench their thirst at ponds, tanks and water-holes around the village and occasionally take a bath. At 3 p.m. they return to the feeding ground for their evening meal, after which they fly a few kilometres away to roost on the ground near the undulating sand dunes for the night. On moonlit nights the spectacle is particularly striking.

When I was in Kheechan the sight that confronted me was startling. The sand dunes around the village had apparently changed colour, covered as they were by hundreds of cranes. Every few minutes flocks of them were either landing or taking off, and the ground around me and the sky above were both so busy that my eyes had a difficult time keeping track of the comings and goings. The people of the village were in continuous contact with the cranes, and at times I had to rub my eyes to believe the spectacle of birds, man and village.

It is not just at Kheechan that vast numbers of cranes can be seen. In the village of Shikarpura a small expanse of water regularly attracts over two thousand demoiselles,

A pair of great Indian bustards, one of six species of bustard to whom the subcontinent is home.
When the male displays his throat pouch inflates and hangs down like a balloon.

which are zealously protected by the inhabitants. Cranes traditionally symbolize good fortune, and most areas of water in the desert are full of them.

The arid and desert regions of Rajasthan and Gujarat are also favoured by the great Indian bustard, a rare bird which dates back to the Eocene period 40–50 million years ago. At the beginning of the twentieth century it was found across the grass plains and desert regions of the subcontinent, but these fragile habitats were the first to suffer in the race for development. Poaching added fuel to the fire, and bustard numbers declined rapidly. Today the small populations that survive in the Great Indian Desert, largely thanks to the protection provided by local communities, probably total less than a thousand.

Adult male great Indian bustards reach a height of 120 centimetres and weigh 10-15 kilogrammes; females are a little smaller. Their diet includes insects, spiders, small lizards, leaves, pulses and the eggs of ground-nesting birds. They also swallow small stones and pebbles to help grind up the food in their stomach. Males and females tend to live in separate flocks. During breeding, males establish individual territories of about 1 square kilometre, while females turn solitary in order to nest. After mating, the female lays one egg and is solely responsible for incubation and chick rearing.

The subcontinent is home to six species of bustard, the males of which perform spectacular courtship displays to attract females and warn off other males. One of them, the lesser florican, has been known to display 500 times in a single day! The great Indian bustard's displays, accompanied by a deep moaning call, involve much strutting about with the chin feathers puffed out. The throat pouch inflates and hangs down like a balloon in front of the legs.

Another bird of these hot regions is the courser, a long-legged and short-winged bird which roams in groups of ten to twelve. It typically moves in short running spurts, punctuated by stops to pick up grubs or insects. While the Indian courser is quite common, the cream-coloured courser is seldom seen. Its plumage merges perfectly with the desert sands, which is an important part of its survival strategy. At any hint of danger, it freezes on the spot and is almost impossible to locate.

It is amazing how such a rich variety of desert creatures survives in conditions that seem intolerable to most humans. I remember once being caught in a sand storm when the temperature was 45°C. Within minutes the visibility declined rapidly and the wind began to blow with frightening intensity. The entire ground seemed to move and every breath made me choke. In the desert one can never be unaware of the extraordinary power of nature.

The monsoon brings only brief respite to the arid northwest, but for a short while when the rain comes crashing down these cracked parched lands are transformed. The landscape turns green, vegetation sprouts, water-holes fill and dry river beds suddenly start to flow. The fury of the monsoon has an enormous impact right across the subcontinent. In other regions it creates some of the wettest forest known to man, and that is where our journey takes us next.

A tiger watches a pair of chinkara in the dry forests of Ranthambhore. It is the only place where tigers have been known to kill these agile animals of the desert.

OVERLEAF *Thousands of demoiselle cranes spend more than half the year around these sand dunes in the centre of the Thar Desert. They are regularly fed by the people of the village nearby who consider them a symbol of good fortune.*

CHAPTER FIVE

WET FORESTS

IT IS PITCH DARK as I step across the forest floor. Just ahead, a thin ray of light illuminates the darkness enveloped by the sounds of birds and crickets. I turn towards the sky and walk into a tangled mesh of green. I am in a sacred grove called a *kavu*, where people worship both gods and nature. Each of these living fragments of the natural heritage of India is a forest garden meant for the exclusive use of certain deities.

According to Hindu tradition, these patches of forest originated after a battle in what is now Sri Lanka between Rama, an incarnation of the great creator god Vishnu, and his brother Lakshmana against the evil giant Rawana, who had kidnapped Rama's wife. Rama was seriously wounded during the fight and Lakshmana fell near him, apparently dead. The only things that could save the brothers were four medicinal plants that grew far away in the mountains of the Himalaya.

Jambavan, Rama's wise adviser, instructed the faithful Hanuman, the flying monkey god, to seek the life-saving plants. Hanuman flew the 3000 kilometres to the Himalaya, but when he arrived he was unable to decide which were the right plants. In frustration he tore out the whole mountain and carried it back, whereupon Rama and Lakshmana were cured by the mere smell of the plants. Hanuman then lifted the mountain once again, to return it to its original home. During the flight bits of earth fell off the mountain and where these landed the sacred groves and holy forests appeared.

Geologists are more prosaic. It is accepted that India and Sri Lanka once formed part of the same land mass and it seems likely that forests covered large, continuous areas of that mass. So once upon a time, probably over a million years ago, the flora and fauna of the forests of Sri Lanka would have spread through an unbroken chain of forest to Assam in northeastern India, some 18 degrees further north and 13 degrees further east. No one is sure when and how the forests gave way to grasslands: the advent of humans, with their fires and their grazing livestock, would have contributed

The arrival of the monsoon in Kerala in southern India. These huge banks of clouds will slowly travel across the subcontinent enveloping it in torrents of rain.

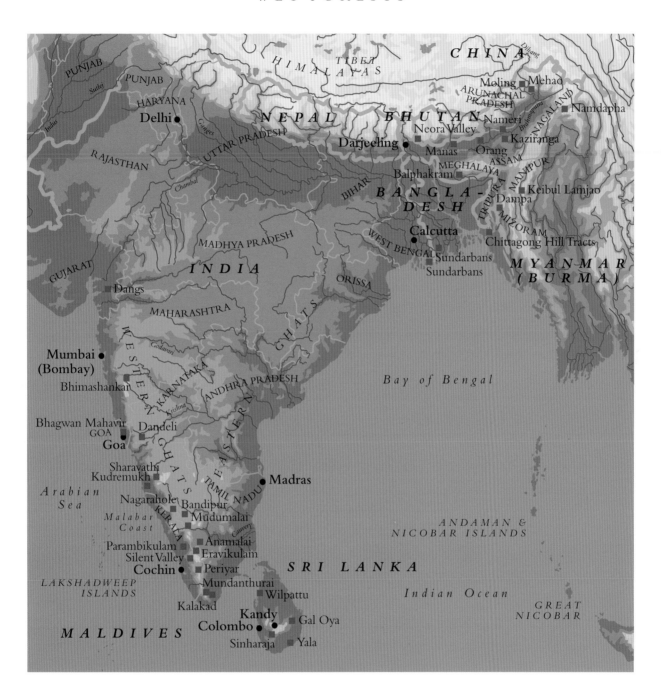

LEFT *Interspersed with grasslands, the moist evergreen forests or sholas of Kudremukh National Park at nearly 2000 metres above sea level are typical of the original forest of the Western Ghats.*

to the destruction of forest, but there is evidence to suggest that the *sholas* existed some 40,000 years ago, long before any human habitation.

But this phase of our journey is concerned with the forests that survive. It takes us to both Sri Lanka and Assam, but concentrates on one of the richest and most beautiful of the forest areas, the Western Ghats, which extend for almost 1600 kilometres down the southwestern side of India, some 200 kilometres inland and parallel to the coast.

Although they receive vast amounts of rain the evergreen forests of the Indian subcontinent are not rainforests in the strictest sense. In the tropical rainforests of the Amazon, for example, rain falls steadily and predictably throughout the year. This ensures that the niches which flora and fauna occupy are always available; and this in turn enables an enormous variety of species to survive. By contrast, in Assam, the driest of our three venues, six months of the year can be classified as a dry season. Yet the sheer volume of rain that falls in the monsoon season – between 1500 mm and 5000 mm in Assam – coupled with the ability of the soil to store moisture, enables these forests to remain green and lush all year round. (To give an idea of just how wet these forests are, London has an average annual rainfall of 600 mm and Los Angeles about 380 mm, less than a quarter of what falls on Assam in a 'dry' year.)

While the diversity of species cannot compare with that of the Amazonian jungles, the subcontinent's wet forests are nevertheless home to at least 50 species of fish, 90 species of amphibian, 44 species of burrowing snake, eight of the 14 pit vipers found in India and 60 species of lizard, not to mention myriad larger fauna such as macaques, langurs, flying squirrels, civets, mongooses, martens, tahr, sambar, bison, leopards and those two great symbols of India, the tiger and the elephant. Sri Lanka also boasts an extraordinary range of jumping spiders, though the tiger has always been absent from this island.

The Western Ghats

The Western Ghats begin as low-lying hills or *dangs* in the northern state of Gujarat, then pass southwards through the states of Maharashtra, Goa, Karnataka and Kerala before ending abruptly in the Mahendragiri Hills at the southern tip of India. Towards that southern end the peak of Anai Mudi, or 'Elephant's Head', rises 2695 metres into the sky. It is the step-like appearance to these mountains which has given them their name: the word *ghats* means the steps of a staircase. Great stretches of moist deciduous and wet evergreen forest cover the Annamalai Hills where the Western Ghats straddle the borders of Tamil Nadu and Kerala, creating breathtaking vistas. There are still 4000 square kilometres of wilderness, much of it now grassland but which, centuries ago, must have been pristine rainforest.

I recently spent some time in Kudremukh National Park in Karnataka, where the Western Ghats climb to a height of over 1800 metres. This area receives torrents of rain annually — up to 7500 centimetres — and is a mosaic of patchy rainforest, known as *shola,* interspersed with open grasslands. The *shola* are montane evergreen forests, supporting species similar to those of the lowland forests, but here the trees are more stunted. Many of the *sholas* grow on steep mountain slopes and the landscape is made the more spectacular by the deep valleys cut through them by perennial rivers. There has been much debate about the origin of these grasslands. Some botanists believe that winter frosts on the slopes limit the growth of woody plants and therefore promote grass. Others conjecture that human settlers cleared parts of the area by regular fires.

A stream flows through the dark, wet vegetation of the Western Ghats.

Studies, however, show that the grasslands existed as much as 40,000 years ago – long before humans inhabited the area – and have always been a special ecological system.

Many hunters have written moving descriptions of the *sholas* and grasslands. One of these was F. W. F. Fletcher, who revealed his enchantment with the area in his book *Sport on the Nilgiris and in Wynaad* (1911).

I reached my destination just as day was breaking, and the view that was unfolded as the sun rose over the rocky ridge behind me I can only call sublime. In front of, and round me, in a semi-circular sweep, the cliffs dropped down to the low country in a sheer unbroken wall. A carpet of green turf ran along the edge, while in every valley and ravine nestled a *shola* of beautiful indigenous trees, running through every shade of colour from dark green to brilliant red. The rhododendrons were in full flower, and the masses of carmine blossom turned each hillside into a garden. Far away below me the plains stretched out to the skyline in an emerald carpet, through which the hill streams wound in bands of silver, sparkling and flashing in the rays of the morning sun. At the foot of the cliffs lay the dense forest which clothes the foothills along the whole western face of the Nilgiris – the home of elephant and bison. To my left, miles away, the needle-like cone of Mukarti shot up into the blue sky, and further still the bold ridge of Nilgiri Peak ran out into the plain, its summit broken into fantastic pillars and cupolas of granite. I know of no sensation to be compared with the feeling of awe that comes over one in the presence of such mighty works of Nature as these. The towering heights; the awful depths; the vast gloomy forest brings home to a man his own insignificance with overwhelming force. And over all broods that tremendous silence; broken only by a stream rippling over the cliffs in a veil of silver, or the swish of a bird's wing as it darts down the sheer drop with a velocity that makes one shudder.

It was so dark and threatening that I decided to make for camp direct. Just as I reached the path along the cliffs, the sable pall split down the centre in front of the sun, and through the rift came a great beam of golden light which bathed everything in its path in glory while all else remained in deepest shadow. 'Heaven peeped through the blanket of the dark.' The effect in such sublime surroundings was magical.

But far more exciting was Fletcher's description of an encounter between a tiger and some Nilgiri tahrs, which he called ibex.

Time passed, and we had a long tramp before us to camp. I was beginning to think we should have to leave the ibex for another day, when suddenly, and as if moved by one impulse, all five sprang to their feet and ran a short way up the cliff. There they stopped, wheeled round, and gazed intently at something below. This manoeuvre was repeated several times, until they reached the landslip.

Under this they huddled for a minute, and then with the peculiar whistle which is the alarm note of the ibex, began to climb rapidly up the broken ground. It was now evident they did not mean to take the track which led past us. Their dark hides showed up clearly against the red earth of the landslip, and the distance could not have been more than two hundred and fifty yards. 'Is it good enough?' whispered J. but I shook my head, for I felt sure we should be able to work round the head of the *shola* in ample time to meet them when they reached the summit of the cliff. With this intention we jumped up and were on the point of starting, when the shikari seized my coat, and pointing down said, 'Pillee, pillee.' The erratic movements of the ibex were now explained, for sure enough, far below us, was a tiger creeping up the face of the cliff, on the line the ibex had taken. With my heart going like a steam pump, I crouched at the edge, expecting every moment to see the tiger's round face appear.

Life in the forest

Rainforests are arranged in a series of tiers. Each tier receives a different amount of light: the tallest trees are bathed in perpetual sunlight, smaller trees and shrubs receive dappled light. The forest floor is in almost complete darkness, full of leaf litter and decaying wood on which mushrooms, lichen and fungi thrive. Early morning visibility can be down to zero till the sun burns off the thick mist.

On the grasslands the temperature can range from 0–30 degrees Celsius in the course of a year; within the forest it remains more or less constant at 15 degrees – another aspect of the predictability and consistency that benefits wildlife.

There is no seasonal leaf fall here; these trees shed their leaves at a slow and steady rate throughout the year, which results in continuous decay and decomposition on the forest floor. This provides a rich environment for the massive buttressed bases of the trees known as dipterocarps, and for a host of smaller life, including termites, leeches and ticks. Indeed, the beetle life is so diverse that all the species have not yet been identified.

The density of growth in these hot and humid jungles is so great that over 70 tall trees can exist in 1 hectare. These trees may be 30–40 metres high and have evolved small, narrow leaves to minimize moisture loss through evaporation. The lower-growing

plants have longer leaves in order to maximize the benefits of the little light that manages to penetrate. At every level, leaves tend to be narrow with drain-like tips so that the monsoon water flows off efficiently. This makes it possible for the leaf to remain relatively dry and 'breathe'.

As I enter the *shola,* the forest floor is dark: somewhere a thin streak of light illuminates a patch of fungi. The atmosphere within is moist and hot. The sky is hidden by the canopy of trees. Suddenly, a great tearing noise interrupts the tranquillity. In the distance a giant tree is falling, taking with it creepers, lianas and other surrounding vegetation. It has survived for centuries, but the moment has come for it to make way for younger trees. Sunlight cascades through the opening in the canopy. It will bring new life as it helps seeds to sprout and saplings to grow – until they are large enough to shade out the sun again and the forest floor returns to darkness.

Everywhere I look there is luxuriant foliage in every shade of green, brilliant orchids, curving and looping lianas, a chaos of tangled growth. Towers of green reach for the sky while moss blankets the dark, cool shade. Ferns, palms, fungi and gnarled fig trees are dappled with light that dances across the forest floor, bouncing away into the high canopy. The frenzy of growth is entwined in a perpetual embrace.

As the sun appears, a great clatter of cicadas starts up. Birds flit around the canopy: imperial pigeons make guttural sounds, emerald doves flash their colours, black-capped kingfishers dip into pools of water, grey jungle fowl flit across the forest path and blue-winged parakeets race across the sky. Dawn is heralded by the call of the Malabar whistling thrush. The orchestra of jungle sounds is completed by the constant calls of the Malabar giant squirrel as it scampers from tree to tree, feeding on flowers and seed pods. A haunting image of these forests is of tigers, drenched in the pouring rain, padding their way along forest paths which can be infested with leeches.

The wind is usually too still to aid in the process of pollination and seed dispersal, which take place through birds, insects, beetles, wasps, butterflies and even monkeys and hornbills. But among the most important pollinators are the bats.

Fruit bat eating a fig. The fruit bat or Indian flying fox is one of the largest of 96 species of bats found in India. It never roosts where it feeds.

Of the 850 species of bats found in the world, 96 occur in India, and all are remarkably adaptable. They have colonized most types of habitat, and are broadly divided into fruit-eaters and insect-eaters. Each performs a vital function: the fruit-eaters digesting seeds and excreting them away from the parent plant so that they can germinate and ensure the survival of their species; the insect-eaters keeping the insect population in check.

But not all of these intriguing mammals are thriving. The fruit bat *Latidens salimalii*, named after the Indian ornithologist Salim Ali and first discovered in the Western Ghats, entered *The Guinness Book of Records* in 1993 as one of the three rarest bat species in the world. Although its favoured habitat is wet evergreen forests, it can also be found in caves, monuments, palaces, forts, ruins and temples, but is now under tremendous pressure as its feeding grounds and habitats dwindle and vanish.

Before the arrival of the monsoon, birds flock to the rainforests to build their nests and breed. When the rains come, armies of insects are created – a feast for the nesting birds. The rains are also greeted by an army of reptiles and amphibians, the first sign of which are flying frogs, which glide through the canopy, their webbed feet outspread. By extending its long fingers and toes a frog creates a parachute effect which helps it glide from tree to tree. These colourful creatures live only in evergreen and moist deciduous forests, and are well adapted to arboreal life. The high canopy provides them with the necessary take-off height to glide between trees – a speedy and energy-saving form of travel.

Flying or draco lizards can soar like butterflies 12 metres or more between trees, spreading their black and orange wing membranes to more than half the length of their bodies. They glide from tall trees to lower elevations and assume vertical positions before landing on a tree trunk. They are entirely arboreal, never touching the ground except while breeding. The breeding season is between February and May, and pre-mating combats between males are frequent, the females remaining passive observers. A courting territory is established and defeated males are chased away from this area. The victor of the combat then nods his head several times at the watching female, stretches his forelegs, folds his throat appendage and shakes it vigorously. Slowly the female moves towards her suitor, then mating starts and continues for eight minutes. It is repeated several times and the pair remain together for the season. The female lays 3–5 white oval eggs, which are buried in the soil. After 50 days the hatchlings break out and are immediately agile, quickly climbing up trees and feeding on ants and other insects.

The Western Ghats are home to dozens of species of amphibians of which 80 per cent are endemic, including the Malabar flying frog.

*The golden tree snake can strike like lightning and even catch prey in mid air.
It is a great 'jumper' between trees and branches.*

Another great climber and jumper in these wet forests is the golden tree snake (*Chrysopelea ornata*). This fascinating creature coils up, then launches its straightened body across a gap between two trees. The movement, which is gliding rather than flying, is achieved by spreading the ribs, flattening the body and sucking in the ventral plates to make them concave. It seems an extraordinary way of avoiding having to deal with perpendicular tree trunks!

Females of the species tend to be larger than males and lay a clutch of 6–12 elongated eggs. Golden tree snakes are diurnal and feed on dracos, geckos, small mammals and birds, which they either kill by constriction or swallow live. They can take prey in mid-air while suspended from a branch: the whole process happens in the blink of an eye. Although these snakes bite viciously, they are not regarded as poisonous.

The tree of life

Perhaps the best way to gain an insight into the life of the forest is to consider a single micro-habitat: the fig tree. There are many species of fig in the rainforests, including the sacred banyan (*Ficus bengalensis*) with its spectacular spreading roots. In a forest of giants, these trees tower the highest. On the upper branches mosses, ferns and even orchids sprout from crevices in the barks. In this thick, tangled growth tree frogs are chased by tree snakes, and bees hum in and out of their hives. Sometimes fig seeds become lodged in the crevices and grow downwards, completely strangling the original tree. There are examples of this strangulation all over the higher parts of the Western Ghats. Lianas root themselves and then climb up to the canopy, providing walkways for the squirrels. Higher up, flying squirrels and lizards glide around defending their .homes and territories, and flying frogs parachute from point to point. If anything deserves to be called 'the tree of life', this is it.

The fig tree has no specific fruiting season: each tree fruits for perhaps 2–3 weeks at a time, but in a large group of trees there will be individuals in fruit at any given time throughout the year. This means, of course, that they are a reliable year-round source of food for a wide variety of animals, from the Nilgiri langurs and bonnet macaques to the tiny and highly specialized fig wasps.

The female fig wasp lays her eggs inside the flower of the fig, guided to receptive flowers by the scent they emit. The flowers are borne inside a globe-shaped inflorescence called a synconium which the wasp must enter through a tiny opening called an ostiole. This is no easy task: forcing her way through the ostiole costs the wasp her wings and sometimes part of her antennae as well. The fig flowers are of two types – long-styled and short-styled – and the female can lay her eggs only in a short-styled flower: her ovipositor is exactly the right length to reach its ovary.

Once inside the synconium, the female deposits her eggs, one in each of about 150 small flowers. About 10 per cent – those containing male larvae – will hatch within a few days. The males are born with mouthparts strong enough to enable them to bite their way out of the flower. Still within the casing of the synconium, they examine the other flowers nearby in search of unhatched females. How they track them down, whether by sight or scent or some mysterious sixth sense, is not known. But these newborn males identify suitable flowers, gnaw holes in them large enough to insert the tip of their abdomen and thus fertilize the females within. They then continue to chew, this time making tunnels that will permit the females (whose mouthparts are much weaker) to leave the synconium. This task completed, the males die and the fertilized females leave the plant of their birth, carrying with them pollen which they deposit on another receptive fig when they lay their eggs and the whole cycle begins again.

In addition to these pollinator wasps, there are a number of different species of parasitic fig wasps, who take advantage of the sophisticated adaptations of their relatives. Female parasitic wasps have much longer ovipositors and are able to lay their

*The great Indian pied hornbill now numbers only a few thousand in the Western Ghats
as more and more mature forests vanish and their nesting trees disappear.*

eggs from outside the synconium. When the young hatch they co-opt the tunnels
created by the male pollinator wasps in order to make their escape to the outside world.

The relationship between the fig tree and the fig wasp is a fascinating one of
mutual dependency and benefit. The wasps have a safe place in which the young can
develop and mate; while the movement of the pollinating wasps from one plant to
another is essential to the propagation and survival of the tree. And the survival of the
fig tree is essential to the wellbeing of the forest and the myriad species that dwell
within it.

The fruit of the fig tree is popular with primates, squirrels and main varieties of
birds. In fact figs constitute 80 per cent of the diet of the king of the forest skies, the

great Indian pied hornbill, although this vulture-sized bird is so powerful that is has also been known to eat flying squirrels.

Wind rushes through the feathers of the hornbill's 120-centimetre wingspan with a loud 'whoosh'. You always hear the pied hornbill, black and white with an immense yellow bill, before you see it; then it sweeps into view like some prehistoric giant. Once common in the wet forests, great pied hornbills now number only a few thousand in two distinct populations: one in about a hundred fragments of forest in and around the Western Ghats, the other in the lower Himalayas and the moist forests of the northeast.

Hornbills also feast on cinnamon and nutmeg. Nutmeg actually relies on the hornbill for seed dispersal since it is a large fruit and can be opened only by birds with a wide gape.

Old fig trees make good homes for hornbills since natural decay creates cavernous holes in the trunks that can easily be turned into nests. Hornbills mate for life, and once they have established a home the pair tend to return to it year after year. They are slow breeders, normally raising only one chick a season. But their meticulous nesting habits are fascinating.

Before the single egg is laid the male and female use their 30-centimetre-long bills as trowels to plaster the female's dried excrement around the nest-hole. The male then seals the nest with the female inside, leaving only a narrow slit through which food may be passed. The female remains inside for three months to incubate the egg and raise her chick. During this time she is fed by the male, who regurgitates figs for her and passes them through the gap in the plaster.

Six weeks after the egg hatches the female breaks out of the nest, leaving the chick to replaster the wall. For another three weeks the male continues to feed the chick, with some help from the female once she has recovered her strength. It is then the turn of the chick to break through the wall and its parents continue to feed it for several more weeks, until it is able to fend for itself.

Humans have often had unfortunate encounters with hornbills: when honey collectors inadvertently disturb their nests, the females have attacked them with their powerful bills.

The lion of the trees

In their quest for fruit, especially figs, giant hornbills are forced to compete with a remarkable primate – the lion-tail macaque. My first glimpse of this 'lion of the trees' was noted in my diary.

Gradually the hills light up in all their splendour and I go to a *shola*. On the way I have a startling glimpse of Nilgiri langurs as they jump through the trees… black bodies framed in a white mane, whooping in the trees. I notice a shrine on the way and discover that it is to the goddess of the *shola*; her blessings are required to keep the peace between man and elephant. Suddenly, a few hundred metres ahead, the forest darkens and a mass of entangled trees creates a dense canopy that the sun finds difficult to penetrate. Below it imperial pigeons cry out and Malabar grey hornbills fly around; overhead the sound of huge wings flapping indicates the presence of great pied hornbills coursing through the sky. The buttressed trunks of huge trees reach for the sky, playing host to numerous epiphytes and orchids, their flowers glinting in the dancing rays of the sun. Rich sounds merge with the entangled branches… The earth is damp, full of leeches and ticks. At the slightest hint of heat, the leeches move in to attack and gorge themselves on blood. Suddenly my thoughts are interrupted by a soft murmur from the trees beyond. I quickly realize that it is the near-human sound of the lion-tail macaque… Its squat shape and face give it an appearance of age and wisdom. I watch at least 20 of them moving in the trees, plucking leaves and licking all the insects off them.

The next morning I spend 40 minutes watching their courtship and mating as they leap across the canopy. A young female follows the dominant male, stopping frequently to cuddle. Unexpectedly, they pause on a branch, cuddle each other and mate. Seconds later, with a big leap, the male jumps from one tree to another, followed by the female. He licks the insects off a leaf and allows it to drop to the forest floor. Slowly other members of the troop leap across to follow the dominant male. In the distance the loud whooping of a troop of Nilgiri langurs breaks the silence.

Near my feet small frogs jump across the damp leaves. A little way ahead a giant gaur stands framed below the trees. Bear faeces indicate the density of sloth bears in this area. Then, in a patch of soft mud, I discover a tiger's pugmark. The lion-tail macaque has no shortage of exciting companions.

Lion-tail macaques are delightful little creatures, distinguished by the mane-like growth around their face and the tuft on the tail that gives them their name. Their life is

Lion-tail macaques are highly endangered, now numbering less than 4000. They fear attacks from the crested hawk eagle that swoops into the canopy after their young.

devoted to the search for food and they spend much of their time feeding in the upper forest canopy. They have an extraordinarily varied diet encompassing over 100 plant species; although they live mainly on seeds, nectar, gum and resin, and are particularly partial to figs, mangoes, small berries, flowers, mushrooms, lichen and mosses, they also eat insects, caterpillars, pupae, spiders, bark insects such as termites, eggs, snails, lizards, small mammals and birds. Adult macaques raid tree-holes to devour eggs, and also steal the young from giant squirrel nests.

This diverse diet means that lion-tails have a different kind of stomach from other macaques: it can digest sugar and carbohydrates but not leaves. This adaptation explains why the species survives only in tropical rainforests, where its mixed diet is readily available.

Lion-tails live in troops of 15–35 individuals, usually covering a range of 1.5–5 square kilometres. A troop consists of 5–10 adult females and their offspring of various ages, ruled over by a single adult male who will mate with any receptive females. Females give birth once every three years, a much lower rate than other macaques, and will probably produce four young in a lifetime. Males are evicted from the troop when they approach maturity and must seek out a territory of their own.

The receptivity of the female – known as the oestrus period – is indicated by a lemon-sized swelling at the base of her tail, which lasts for about 14 days out of a cycle of about 45 days. In one study in the Western Ghats it was observed that the females did not come into oestrus at all during March and April – the driest time of the year – although there were also 'peak' periods during the monsoon season when most or all of the mature females in a troop become receptive simultaneously. Mating is frequently interrupted or even prevented altogether by other females harassing the mating pair, either chasing away the chosen female, pulling the male's tail to prevent him mounting, or simply standing in the way. Often the male will then mate with this new female – which is presumably what she was trying to achieve!

Around 20,000 years ago rainforests covered most of peninsular India and lion-tails would have roamed far and wide. Since then, however, tectonic plate movements have pushed the peninsula further north from the Equator, relegating the rainforests to the southern edges of the Western Ghats and thereby ensuring that this became the final home of the lion-tail macaque. Today, owing to encroachment from tea and coffee estates, the lion-tails' habitats are highly fragmented and they live only in the higher elevations. The total population is probably 4000 animals – 1000 each in the states of Karnataka and Tamil Nadu, and 2000 in Kerala.

The Nilgiri tahr or 'cloud goat' is at home in the craggy inclines and rocks of the Western Ghats.

Other residents of the Western Ghats

The wet forests of the Western Ghats are also home to a leaf-eating primate, the Nilgiri langur. It takes its name from the Nilgiri Hills, a range within the Ghats which overlaps the borders of Karnataka, Tamil Nadu and Kerala. Although it does not have to compete with the macaque for food, it will react ferociously if forced into the same tree or if its infants are threatened. Normally it contents itself with loud vocal protest and then retreats, but there are occasions when the fight can be frenzied. Ajith Kumar, a wildlife biologist who has studied lion-tails for years, described one such encounter.

Turning around, I saw the lion-tail male hurrying to the ground and disappearing among the thick undergrowth, while the other monkeys of the group stood staring down, growling and wailing. Within seconds, the male was going up the same tree, but with a Nilgiri langur infant clutched in his mouth. While the other monkeys growled and wailed even more excitedly, he went up about 5 metres, stood with the infant in his mouth for a couple of minutes, then dropped it to the ground. I could see drops of blood on his white mane. As the male sat down licking his bloody hand, two adult females came running to him excitedly and started grooming him. The growling and wailing continued for a few seconds more, then there was only the sound of the cicadas. The Nilgiri langurs looked on from about 50 metres' distance before slowly moving away. About five minutes later, the lion-tail macaques also started drifting away. We examined the infant langur on the ground. It was dead, but still warm and had deep canine marks on the chest and neck.

At dawn the loud booming call of the Nilgiri langurs echoes through the rainforests. They thrive in the *sholas* and live mainly at altitudes of 900–2000 metres. Troops vary in size from three to 25, with an adult male leading the group. As a specialist leaf-eater the langur has evolved an unusual two-part stomach which allows it to digest foliage more efficiently than any other primate. Food passes first through the upper part of the stomach, where anaerobic bacteria break down the cellulose in the leaves in order to release energy. The bacteria also neutralize the many toxic compounds found in the leaves, enabling the langur to feed safely on a wide range of leaf types. In the lower region of the stomach, acid completes the process of digesting the toxin-free food.

The Nilgiri langur, like the lion-tail macaque, is endemic to this region.

The Nilgiri langur, which is glossy black in colour, has been widely hunted for its beautiful fur, and for its flesh, blood and organs, which are supposed to have medicinal properties. Little wonder it is under serious threat of extinction.

The Nilgiri tahr, a member of the goat family, lives high in the Western Ghats, where it has been nicknamed the 'cloud goat' because it is often seen moving in and out of mist, fog and cloud. The ancestors of the tahr are supposed to have originated in the later stages of the Pleistocene period, which ended 10,000 years ago. Some 1500–2000 Nilgiri tahrs survive, confined to a 400-kilometre stretch of hills in the southern portion of the Western Ghats. As grazers needing a constant supply of food, they enjoy the grasslands that hug the rocky cliffs above 1200 metres, but they also like the *sholas,* which provide shade and shelter during their seasonal wanderings. They share these areas with elephant, gaur, sambar and barking deer. Tahrs do most of their feeding during the early morning and the evening; during the hot hours of the day, they shelter in the shade of crags and rocks, one member of the group acting as look-out in order to warn of any approaching danger, which may take the form of leopards, wild dogs or even tigers.

For most of the year tahrs tend to live in segregated groups: the adult males in bachelor herds, the females and young in separate family parties. Only during the breeding season (between June and September) do the two groups mix. Males, who have white facial stripes, a distinct patch of white fur on their backs, and thick horns that curve backwards, fight for the females not just by crashing their horns into each other, but by barging into each other's flanks, shoulder to shoulder. The young are born after a gestation period of six months, and are quickly weaned off milk and on to grass. If a female's offspring dies, she quickly conceives again – an ability that has probably played a vital part in the survival of Nilgiri tahr populations.

Another remarkable and endemic species of these forests is the Nilgiri marten, a weasel-like creature with prominent ears, an inquisitive face and short, powerful limbs which enable it to run swiftly up vertical tree trunks. Although extremely agile when hunting in trees, it arches its spine when running on the ground, so looks surprisingly clumsy. Rarely seen below 900 metres, the Nilgiri marten is essentially carnivorous, pursuing rats, mice, hares, mouse deer, partridges and pheasants on the ground and birds and squirrels in the trees. It also raids nests, feeding on the eggs.

The marten shares the forest canopy with the Indian giant squirrel, sometimes

A Malabar giant squirrel squeezes past bonnet macaques to feast on the jack fruit.
The wet forests of Periyar in Kerala are some of the finest in the region.

called the Malabar giant squirrel. Reaching a length of 1 metre, including the tail, these squirrels evolved some 10-25 million years ago and now inhabit the deciduous, mixed deciduous and moist evergreen forests of peninsular India. They make their homes in the tallest trees 30-40 metres above the ground and wake at dawn to greet the day with a loud rattling call that echoes across the enormous canopy. Giant squirrels tend to feed in the morning and the late afternoon, spending the time in between nest-building and chasing intruders away from food trees.

During courtship males compete for a female's attention, and it is up to her to choose a mate. She has a single pup which spends the first year of its life in the tree in which it is born. Mother and pup often play together, an activity which both obviously enjoy and which is a delight to watch. After a year a pup will leave the tree to make its own nest and become independent.

Giant squirrels are alert to any kind of danger, and their alarm call rattles across the forest canopy at the sight or sound of something unusual. I once heard a forest explode with alarm when these squirrels heard a leopard call from the distance.

Sinharaja

So far we have concentrated on a single area of wet forest, the Western Ghats, but our journey has yet to take us to the extreme south and the extreme north of the Indian subcontinent. First, to the south and to the forest of Sinharaja in Sri Lanka.

Sinharaja, at only 6 degrees north of the Equator, is more truly tropical rainforest than the Western Ghats and supports a wider variety of species, many of which are unique to the area. The Sinharaja forest reserve covers 8500 hectares — a tiny fragment of primeval rainforest unique on the Indian subcontinent. The fact that Sri Lanka is an island increases the occurrence of unique (or endemic) species, but so too does the rainfall: it has been suggested that endemism is at its peak where rainfall is greatest. For example, the Sri Lankan forests contain 45 species of the group of trees known as dipterocarps. An impressive enough figure on its own, but of these a staggering 44 are endemic.

Many fascinating animals live in the canopy created by the trees. They include the purple-faced leaf monkey and the toque macaque, a subspecies of the bonnet macaque. Mouse deer, barking deer and sambar deer graze below and are preyed on by Sinharaja's largest carnivore, the leopard. Rusty spotted cats and fishing cats are also found in the area.

Brightly coloured birds such as the Ceylon magpie, Layard's parakeet and the green-billed coucal with its beautiful, bubbling call can be seen flitting through the foliage. The rare red-faced malkoha may also occasionally be seen. Sri Lanka is a

The three-toed kingfisher, a bird of the wet forests, is solitary by nature;
it is found in and around pools of water.

OVERLEAF *Sri Lanka's rainforests have some of the finest trees.*
Much of this vegetation is endemic to this island.

birdwatcher's paradise, with over four hundred species, either resident or migratory visitors, many of them apparently equally happy around human habitation as in more remote areas.

Among its forty-five species of reptile, Sinharaja boasts two unique lizards, the rough leaf-nosed and the hump-nosed. The hump-nosed lizard lives in trees and is found only in undisturbed rainforests. Competition among males – for females and territory – is impressive and aggressive, but manages to avoid actual combat. When challenged, a male changes colour, exposes sharp teeth and raises its crest. One or other of the rivals in such an encounter usually backs down. One of the many species

An exquisitely coloured jumping spider. Its displays include elaborate dancing and leg-waving in its efforts to attract the opposite sex.

of jumping spider is less prudent: the male *Myrmarachne plataleodes* can unfold huge fangs when he wants to joust with other males.

The jumping spiders occupy every niche in the forest from floor to canopy. Around the world they are found from the depths of the Dead Sea to some 5000 metres up Mount Everest, and from seashore to desert. Jumping spiders have exceptional vision: their eight eyes, which give them peripheral vision similar to that of humans as well as strong forward vision like most larger predators, occupy more space than their brain in their body. They can detect motion all around and distinguish details at distances of twenty times their body length. Scientists are baffled by this: such highly developed vision, with all its implications for complex behaviour, shouldn't exist in a creature with such a tiny brain!

Jumping spiders communicate through a series of displays, including dancing and leg waving. Males also use these displays to attract mates. Because they rely so much on sight, they have evolved some eye-catching physical features: the different species boast multicoloured hair tufts, manes, moustaches, beards and 'hairstyles' in colours that few other creatures can rival.

In Sri Lanka, the iridescent *Chrysilla* lives in the treetops and the male uses his rainbow colours to attract a mate, raising his body and rotating his abdomen in the air. Courtship is prolonged, with the female alternately approaching the male and then retreating. Bizarrely, the courtship ritual we watched ended not with mating but with the male eating the female! This happened four or five times, and the expert we consulted was unable to explain it.

Portia labiata is perhaps the most cunning of the jumping spiders. It preys on web spiders and hunts in the lower reaches of the forest, among the dark buttresses of the dipterocarps. First establishing how big and how far away the prey spider is by plucking on the edge of the web, it then plucks the web more vigorously in order to appear like a struggling victim. If the spider advances towards it, *Portia* then changes its behaviour, either turning around to approach from another direction or stalking its victim with a curious robot-like motion. After such an elaborate build-up, the attack is startlingly quick and efficient.

Portia has also been known to disguise itself as a piece of detritus so that it can lurk undetected on its victim's web. It then waits for a gust of wind to disturb the web so that it can move forward under cover of the movement caused by the wind. But in the dense forest where wind is slight, this is an unreliable technique, so *Portia* has also developed the tactic of making an occasional large vibration to disguise its usual small ones. It can also imitate the sound of a falling twig: its prey will not then be alarmed to see it landing on the web.

Wet forests of northeastern India

Some 1500 kilometres away from the Western Ghats, in northeastern India, is another area of wet forest where many similar species are to be found. One area, in the state of Meghalaya, receives some of the highest rainfall on the subcontinent.

Here, among the Khasi Hills, are 1000 square kilometres of *kavus*, some of which have survived untouched through fear of the deities to which they are dedicated. Indeed, the Mawsmal grove in the town of Cherrapunji is believed to be inhabited by a powerful and malicious spirit who prescribes death for those who destroy or damage the forest. The spirit can be appeased only by the sacrifice of a male goat.

Cherrapunji is one of the wettest places on the subcontinent. The average rainfall is 1200 centimetres but in one astonishing year there was 2400 centimetres of rain, with up to 100 centimetres falling in a single day. This is as much as New York gets in a year! Cherrapunji receives this rainfall because it sits at the end of a 'funnel' formed by two mountain ranges. Moist winds off the Bay of Bengal pour into the funnel, picking up moisture from warm flood waters. As the passage narrows, these winds rise and cool. The moisture then condenses and falls in a torrent of rain.

In prehistoric times the northeast region of the subcontinent served as a gateway through which oriental fauna could spread to India. The natural barrier of the Himalayas and the formation of the Thar Desert in the northwest made passage by other routes immensely difficult. Wildlife is believed to have passed down peninsular India and beyond by way of various forest habitats. Subsequent geological and climatic changes, however, 'locked' animals into particular areas and prevented further dispersal. For this reason, certain species found mainly in the Western Ghats have close relatives which are found only in the northeast, in Meghalaya and Assam.

Among the creatures the wet forests of northeast and southwest have in common is the clawless otter, found in the Western Ghats, the Himalayan foothills from Kulu eastwards to Arunachal Pradesh, and in the plains of Assam and lower Bengal. A great swimmer, it feeds on fish, snails, mussels, crabs and other aquatic creatures.

As further evidence of the ancient link, martens, squirrels, great pied hornbills and Malabar pied hornbills occur in both northeast and southwest. There are related species such as the Malabar and Himalayan civets, Nilgiri and Himalayan yellow-throated martens, lion-tail and pig-tail macaques, and so on. All share basic characteristics but have adapted in slightly different ways to their specific environment.

The richly life-supporting fig tree is also common to the rainforests of north and south. In Assam it is the principal source of food for a species that is endemic to the area, the hoolock gibbon. India's only ape spends up to 60 per cent of its time searching for

*The hoolock gibbon is India's only ape. They pair for life and zealously guard
their homes, fearing attack especially from the clouded leopard.*

and feeding on figs. In the heat of the day hoolocks rest in the cool, shady part of the
canopy, where they lick or sip the dew from moisture-laden leaves. Hoolocks, which
stand less than 1 metre high and weigh 6-8 kilogrammes, are the most agile of primates
and seem almost to fly from tree to tree. They feed on young leaves, buds, leaves, flowers
and fruit at the very top of the canopy, where their weight can cause them to teeter
precariously amid the thin branches and even to slide off. To combat this problem they
have learned to hang by both hands and feet, their long arms enabling them to distribute
their weight over several supports so that they can feed more safely.

Hoolocks pair for life and live in monogamous family groups, each consisting of an adult pair with their offspring. The young, born at different times, will stay with their parents until the age of seven or eight. A pair occupies a territory of 20–40 hectares, which it defends zealously with a loud, shrill duet sung out especially in the morning.

The principal predator of the wet northeastern forest is the rarely seen clouded leopard, so named because of the cloudy spots that cover its coat. It is found across the forests of Southeast Asia, extending eastwards from Nepal to southern China and southwards to Malaysia, Sumatra and Borneo. Weighing 16–23 kilogrammes, it stands 45 centimetres tall, measures 1.2–1.8 metres in length and has canines that are nearly 4.5 centimetres long. Its short legs and large feet give it a low centre of gravity, which ensures an excellent grip on tree branches. The four main digits are webbed and have double claw sheaths, so the claws are retractable.

When hunting, clouded leopards often spring to the ground from tree overhangs and use small shrubs or branches as camouflage. Known locally as *sebegyar,* or 'one who catches monkeys', they prey on primates such as the hoolock gibbon, plus snakes and smaller animals that frequent the canopy. Before feeding they use their rasp-like tongue to clean feathers and fur off their prey.

The golden cat has been hunted mercilessly for its fur, but tiny populations
still survive in the dense wet forests of the northeastern region.

*The life in the wild of the clouded leopard is a mystery. Seldom seen,
but intensively poached, this elusive predator is probably entirely arboreal.*

Local people believe the clouded leopard rears its young in the vast hollows of
trees, using the horizontal boughs as its pathways across the canopy. Some claim that it is
entirely arboreal and catches all its prey in the crowns of forest trees. It is certainly well
adapted to such a life, as it can jump 5 metres and more between trees, run head-first
down tree trunks, climb while upside-down and hang from branches by its hind feet.
On a few small islands off Sabah it is also known to swim well and even to catch fish.

Also rare and seldom seen is the golden cat, which inhabits the thick evergreen
forests found across Nepal, Sikkim, Assam and into Burma. It has a dark golden-brown

coat and reaches over 1.2 metres in length. Its most conspicuous feature, however, is a white cheek stripe that runs below the eye. Little is known of the golden cat's habits, but it has the agility and strength to prey on small deer, goats, sheep and even buffalo calves. Some people believe that it hunts on the forest edges in rocky outcrops; others maintain that, like the clouded leopard, it lives in the trees.

Another arboreal creature of the northeastern rainforests is the binturong, more commonly known as the bear cat. Related to the African civet, this species has a body length of 75 centimetres, and a large bushy tail which can extend to over 60 centimetres. The tail, together with its tufted ears and shaggy coat, gives it a rather grizzled appearance. It sleeps in trees and starts moving at dusk, when its tail is a great help in climbing up and down. In fact, the young support themselves entirely by the tail in their first months of life. Bear cats prey on the small animals, birds, insects and fruits that they find in the forest canopy, but little else is known of these mysterious creatures.

The evergreen wet forests are unique reserves of life on Earth, and these living fragments of our prehistoric past produce fascinating insights into the evolution of our planet. Now, however, having journeyed up mountains, across the flood-plains to the sea, through deserts and forests, we enter the regions where people have for many centuries lived alongside our most fearsome predator.

LEFT *The elusive binturong or bear cat uses its large bushy tail to help it negotiate the dense forest canopy.*

OVERLEAF *Elephants in Sri Lanka. Torrents of rain pour down on these wet forests, creating a very special habitat for a rich array of wildlife.*

CHAPTER SIX

THE TIGER'S DOMAIN

As a boy looking at pictures and hearing stories of tigers I developed a great urge to see one in the forests of India. I still remember that early morning in Corbett National Park in 1961 when, at the age of nine, I got on top of an elephant in search of a tiger. The grasslands were enveloped in mist and I remember my hands were numb with cold as three elephants swept through the high grasses serching for a tigress and her cubs. My heart raced in anticipation of seeing a tiger. I was jolted out of my stupor when a barking deer exploded in alarm a few metres from the elephants. Suddenly a tigress with two 'dog'-sized cubs rushed past with a snarl. It was a scene I will never forget. It was fifteen years later that I saw my next tiger, in Ranthambhore National Park in Rajasthan, which to me was the great jewel in the tiger's domain. It was to be for me the beginning of my quest to understand not just the tiger but a host of other wildlife that shares this fragile land of the tiger.

I want to share with you some of the most memorable moments that I have had both with tigers and other animals and which are still vivid in my mind. In Ranthambhore I witnessed an encounter between a tigress called Noon and a sambar deer that is still vivid in my mind. My diary notes for that day recall the event:

From where the tigers had disappeared, gallops one of the largest sambar stags I have ever seen, closely pursued by Noon. Does Noon expect to kill such a large stag in a chase over open ground? Stag and tigress are out of sight some 30 metres ahead. Fumbling with the starter of the jeep, I move on, heart pounding. A couple of metres from the vehicle track the stag stands motionless in a clearing. Noon clings to the side of its neck. The tiger's canines have a grip, but they are nowhere near the throat. Both tiger and sambar are frozen in this

The fragile wilderness of Ranthambhore at dawn. Scattered throughout the forest are remnants of temples and palaces where centuries ago royal courts flourished. Today it is nature's own paradise.

position, staring at each other. There is not a sound or a movement. I am so close that I feel I could touch them. Noon seems unwilling to shift her grip, which might allow the sambar to escape. A few parakeets fly overhead and some green pigeons chatter in a tree nearby as tiger and sambar remain locked together.

In a few minutes the sambar, with a great heave of his neck, shrugs the tigress off, but in a flash she attacks his forelegs in an effort to break them. The stag jerks away, but Noon goes again for the neck, rising on her haunches with one paw on his shoulder for leverage. The sambar swivels around and Noon now attacks his belly. After much struggling, the sambar finds himself in a sitting

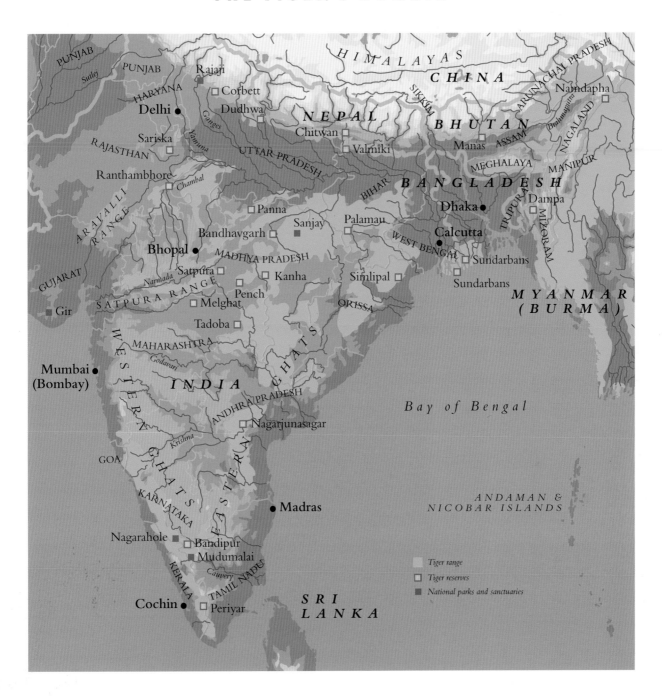

LEFT *A tigress locked in combat with a sambar deer. The tigress has failed to get a grip on the deer's throat and now tries desperately to wrestle it down.*

OVERLEAF *A tigress snatches the carcass of a sambar deer from the crocodiles in Ranthambhore's lake. Her cubs watch in anticipation of the feast.*

position, while the tigress takes a firm grip on one of his hind legs. Noon's male cub appears and stands motionless, observing the encounter. Noon and sambar are again frozen in position. The cub inches closer, perhaps sensing victory. Noon yanks at the hind leg, trying desperately to break it. This is the only way she will prevent the stag from escaping, as her grip is not a fatal one. I am totally mesmerized. The cub must be learning a lot from watching the combat.

Suddenly, the sambar, utilizing every ounce of his strength, shakes Noon off, stands and runs. The cub flees in fear and an exhausted Noon tries to chase the sambar. The stag, with a burst of adrenalin, escapes in the direction from which he came. Noon lopes after him, but hasn't the energy to sustain any speed. Her cubs gather around, as if egging her on, but she snarls at them in irritation. The cubs run ahead of her, following the sambar to the water's edge. The stag alarm-calls for the first time, a strange, dull, hollow sound, as if his vocal chords have been damaged in the attack. Seeing the approaching tigers, he wades into the lake. Noon and her cubs watch anxiously from the shore. The stag has great difficulty moving through the water. He stumbles forward and finds himself in a deep patch; he is forced to swim and nearly drowns. His head bobs up and down, his limbs move frantically as he struggles to reach the far bank. The tigers follow along the shore, but Noon soon gives up and reclines at the edge, exhausted and panting. Her tongue is cut and bleeding.

What enormous power and impact tigers have. No wonder they were worshipped!

Kipling country

Our journey has brought us full circle, back to the heart of India where so many of the sacred creatures we considered in the introduction are found. We are in Madhya Pradesh – Kipling country. This is the land of the *Jungle Books*, where the descendants of Shere Khan the tiger still prowl. For many observers, Madhya Pradesh is the true land of the tiger; not only does it have the highest tiger population in India, it also has some of the most exciting habitats anywhere in the tiger's range. These include the steep ledges that look down on the raging Ken River in Panna, the exquisite bamboo forests of Bandhavgarh, the open meadows of Kanha and the rolling highlands of Satpura. Here, in Satpura the river meanders around looming cliffs, creating landscapes of infinite beauty. Barking deer watch you pass, paralysed for a few seconds, before bounding away; sambar seem immense and dark with coats that look like velvet. Sheltered under enormous trees, 10–15 kilometres apart, are old rest-houses created by

A tigress carefully watches the attack of a marsh crocodile on a sambar deer.
At the opportune moment she will hope to scavenge the carcass from the crocodile.

the British administration and sometimes used today by animal observers. Highlands and lowlands merge in Madhya Pradesh and several rivers split the area into excellent riverine habitats where density of predators and prey is high.

In my diary I recorded my impressions of my first visit to this lovely place:

Giant squirrels in the canopy of the trees hop from branch to branch and tree to tree; racquet-tail drongos shrill loudly and flash their peculiar tails; everywhere one senses the presence of the tiger and expects to encounter it around each corner...

A chilly winter's morning, and as I wind the jeep down the road, I spot tiger pugmarks. A large tigress has walked the forest track accompanied by at least three cubs 12-14 months old. The track is criss-crossed with pugmarks where the cubs have run back and forth and all around their mother. The tracks continue for nearly 7 kilometres over a plateau and into a steep valley – then they vanish.

At the end of a sharp descent the forest opens on to a magical river of sparkling, gurgling water, its emerald green depths full of fish darting around.

Leopards are relegated to cliffs, hills and rocky outcrops when they share the forest with the tiger. Many tigers have attacked and eaten leopards in confrontations.

Sharp rocky cliffs carry their bamboo forests up to the sky. Here, barking deer appear and disappear, large herds of gaur clatter around and sambar peer alertly at the human intruders. High above are numerous nests of giant Malabar squirrels, which share the space with pied and grey hornbills. Tentative leopard pugs reflect their anxiety in the tiger's domain. Indian sloth bears abound in these hills, making their homes in rock crevices and caves.

Also found on the hot plains, sloth bears can weigh over 135 kilogrammes and reach a length of 1.5 metres. They have been known to live to the age of forty. Their main food is termites, but they love honey, which they raid from the nests of large rock bees. They are also voracious fruit-eaters, but sometimes feed on carrion and have been known to chase tigers off kills – although it must be admitted that the tiger usually comes off better in these encounters.

The Indian sloth bear has the remarkable capacity to carry its young on its back for safety. Sloth bear mothers protect their young zealously.

Sloth bears are characterized by their long, unkempt hair and the white V-shaped patch on their breast. They shelter in rocky outcrops and crevices where tumbled boulders have created natural dens. Mating and courtship take place during hot weather and the young are born in winter. The mother carries very young cubs on her back and protects them fiercely till they mature. I have often witnessed a wrathful mother bear charging a jeep or a man on foot, and on one occasion chasing away a tiger.

Throughout the tiger's range, the peace of the day or night may suddenly be interrupted by the alarm call of a bird, antelope or monkey. In deep forest the sentinel is likely to be a barking deer or muntjac. Having sensed the tiger's presence, it warns other animals of impending danger. Secretive and solitary, this tiny creature carries both antlers and the over-developed canines or *tushes* which many deer use as weapons of attack or defence.

In Satpura the gaur or giant ox looms large. It weighs over a tonne and lives in the wet forests of southern and northeastern India. In Satpura there are four totally white gaur – presumably albinos or some genetic sport – who, amid their black companions, appear like ghosts in a forest!

The sambar is among the tiger's favourite prey. Largest of the Asiatic deer, it is found throughout the tiger's domain, from the dry deciduous forests of Rajasthan to the semi-evergreen and evergreen forests of the Western Ghats and Assam. Standing 1.5 metres at the shoulder and weighing more than 270 kilogrammes, sambars congregate in small groups, which adult males join only when a female is in oestrus. Courtship and mating occur during the winter months, when stags fight aggressively for the favours of the females; the young are born just after the monsoon. For tiger watchers the alarm call of this deer is a definite indication that a predator is nearby.

The dry and moist deciduous forests of Satpura are home to thousands of sambar, and late in the evening their loud, booming call resonates across these highlands. Sambars are good swimmers and relish the water, especially during the hot summer months. They also enjoy feeding on aquatic plants: in Ranthambhore there is a resident population in and around the lakes.

India's largest antelope inhabits drier territory and may also be found around waterholes in the desert. This is the nilgai or blue cow. It earns its English name through a vague resemblance to the domesticated cow; and although the two species are not

PREVIOUS PAGES *Gaur, the largest of the world's wild oxen, can be nearly three times the body weight of an adult tiger, yet the experienced tiger has been known to predate successfully on these giants.*

Young tigers up to the age of 16 months can climb trees and rest on the branches.
Soon after this age their body weight becomes too heavy for the tree to support.

OVERLEAF *Nilgai or great Indian antelope are sacred right across India. The 'blue cow',*
as it is known, has flourished in and out of forests and is an important prey species for the tiger.

*Wild dogs work as a pack and have been known to chase leopards
and sometimes even tigers from their kills.*

related, the nilgai has benefited from the same veneration as the familiar 'sacred cow'.
As a result its numbers are increasing and in some areas it is regarded a nuisance, but it
is still tolerated because of its name.

The nilgai is a substantial creature with disproportionately small horns. However,
rival males can still inflict serious wounds on each other during the rutting season. The
rut is a ritualized affair, with the males arching their necks, holding their tails erect and
stalking round each other in small circles before dropping to their knees and engaging
in combat. In principle the successful male earns the exclusive right to mate with the
females of a group, but in practice vanquished males have been known to sneak in and
mate while the dominant male is busy dealing with other challengers.

Living in small groups, the nilgai relies on the vigilance of the matriarchs of the herd to alert the others to any scent or sound of danger. The first warning is given by the stamp of a foot, followed by an alarm call and, if necessary, a hasty retreat. Again, this stampede alerts all the other potential prey species in the area to the presence of danger.

In the Satpura mountains the wild boar is another vital part of the tiger's diet, the young being most vulnerable. Adult males can charge and swerve around at lightning speed, and many a tiger has retreated from the ferocity of the attack. Some have even been killed.

From time to time packs of wild dogs in groups of anything from three to twenty slip into the area to attack and feast. These whistling coursers are feared by all the denizens of the Indian jungle; a silent forest will explode into a cacophony of alarm calls when a pack is spotted on the move. Even tigers will desert their kills if a pack of dogs threatens them. The spotted deer or chital is the dogs' favourite prey; they surround, attack and tear it apart with consummate efficiency.

The Bengal tiger's domain still stretches over most of the Indian subcontinent. The westernmost point of its habitat is the edge of the desert in Ranthambhore. This dry, deciduous belt is very different from the moist deciduous forests of Madhya Pradesh where tigers thrive in bamboo forests. Further south, in the rainforests of Tamil Nadu and Kerala, they can survive at altitudes of 1800 metres. To the north, in Bhutan, they are found up to 3500 metres, and recent reports from southeastern Tibet suggest that they have been tracked as high as 4500 metres. Tigers flourish among the thick ever-green forests of the northeast and on the *terai* grasslands, where there is plenty of prey. As we have seen, one of the largest populations of tigers is found at the edge of the sea in the inaccessible mangrove swamps of the Sundarbans in West Bengal. Only in open arid regions are tigers unable to survive.

In fact, I have done most of my tiger-watching in Ranthambhore, which has been my second home for over twenty years. Ranthambhore National Park includes a variety of habitats within its 400 square kilometre area – dry deciduous forest, rolling hills, open grasslands and a number of substantial lakes. It is ideal tiger country and a place to absorb the secret life of tigers.

A large male tiger weighs about 200 kilogrammes, an average female perhaps 150. The striped coat is ideal camouflage in the dappled shade of the forest and this combined with their finely tuned stalking techniques enables them to approach very close to prey before making their presence known with a final powerful rush. Like most cats tigers kill their prey with a single decisive bite – usually to the throat in the case of large animals, to the back of the neck with smaller ones. They have excellent night vision and are most active between dusk and dawn, but they will hunt whenever they can. Never sure when they are going to be able to kill again, they are capable of eating vast amounts at one time, as much as 50–80 kilogrammes of meat in three or four days. In fact, tigers, for all their stealth and strength, fail in nine out of ten hunting attempts, and get no second chance – their attack alerts every prey animal within earshot, and they are too heavy to run after a fleeing animal for long.

It has been estimated that an adult tiger needs about 1800–2500 kilogrammes of meat a year, which means it must kill a medium-sized animal about once a week. A female with cubs to feed must do better than this – she needs to kill about once every five days. A tiger will drag its kill into the nearest cover to protect it from vultures and other scavengers; once it has glutted itself it will move on, patrolling its range until it is time to hunt again.

As tiger cubs are born blind and helpless, tigresses in Ranthambhore select the safest and thickest part of the forest as their home. The forest is also rich in prey species and provides plenty of water – critical ingredients to sustain mother and cubs in the first few months. Those early days, when the tigress suckles her young, hunts for herself and licks and cajoles the tiny cubs into life, are not only exhausting but must be racked with tension about possible predators. The tigress hides her cubs in a den, and is ruthless in her protection of them, seldom allowing even the possibility of human observation. If there is the slightest disturbance, she will change dens, carrying her helpless cubs to their new refuge one by one in her mouth.

The cubs grow rapidly in the first month, becoming frisky and bold. They start to explore the area around their den, and indulge in constant games of licking, jumping, nibbling, pawing and playing with their tails. They also establish a teat order, which eventually leads to a hierarchy among them. The tigress instils a sense of order and discipline by the occasional snarl, cough or growl. I have a record of watching a tigress with three cubs around her:

One nuzzles her face, another rests on her back, the third watches me, tries to stalk forward, then rapidly retreats to its mother. The cubs then turn and swat each other, leaping high into the air. They dash towards their mother, who licks one of them and then decides to lie on her side to suckle them. All three soon find the right teat and feed, stimulating the flow of milk by pummelling with their tiny paws.

The legendary tiger Genghis (see pages 92–3), who endlessly predated on young sambar deer in the waters of Ranthambhore's lakes.

In this case the den was in a gorge 30 metres long and 10 metres wide, surrounded on two sides by a rock overhang 20 metres high. The cubs lived in two small caves in the cliff-face. Dense cover carpeted the floor of the gorge and a large pool of water made the setting ideal.

After two months, the diet of milk is supplemented by meat, which the mother drags or carries to the den. During this time the cubs become more adventurous, nibbling at twigs and branches, and prodding stones and boulders. They absorb new sounds and learn to stand their ground in the absence of their mother. Remnants of kills litter the area around the den, and the cubs chase off crows and tree pies as they peck at the bones. Family life can also include the father, and I was the first to record this fact in the forests of Ranthambhore.

*A rare picture of a tiger family: the resident male with a tigress and
her two young cubs fighting the heat of the day.*

At four in the afternoon Kublai, the resident male tiger, lazily ambles towards
the pool and slides into the water, hind legs first, soaking himself completely,
leaving just his head visible. Tigers don't like water splashing in their eyes –
most of them enter water backwards. About twenty minutes later Nalghati, the
resident female, follows and they both laze around in the water. Minutes later
my heart misses a beat. The male cub walks quite nonchalantly towards the
pool, not a flicker of surprise or fear on his face, circles the two adults and
enters the water near where Kublai is stretched out. Soon, following her
brother, the female cub walks to the pool, entering the water to sit on her
mother's paw. Nalghati licks her face. One big happy family: Nalghati, Kublai

and two five-month-old cubs all in close proximity in this rather small pool of water, which they lap at regular intervals.

After half an hour the male cub rises, quickly nuzzles Kublai and leaves the pool. The female cub follows him and they play, leaping at each other, drifting towards a tree, clambering up the branches to play a game of hide and seek amid the foliage. The two adult tigers watch. Soon Nalghati leaves the water and disappears into the forest. The cubs continue to play under the protective eye of Kublai. At dusk, Kublai heaves himself out of the water and moves towards the cubs. The cubs rush up to him. He licks one of them.

Soon afterwards I noted very similar behaviour in another family group, after I had watched a tigress called Laxmi and her mate, whom we called the Bakaula male, co-operate in killing a sambar.

Laxmi grips the throat of the sambar for a couple of minutes, ensures that there is no life left in it and starts the tedious process of dragging the nearly 150-kilo-gramme carcass away, a few metres at a time, into thick cover. The male watches her carefully and moves forwards. He places his forepaws on the sambar's rump, taking hold of one of the hind legs. Laxmi has a firm grip on the throat. The carcass is stretched between the two tigers. A mock tug of war ensues as each tries to pull the carcass nearer. Both tigers emit low-pitched growls, interspersed with herculean tugs at the carcass. Then, with a sudden burst of energy and strength, Laxmi yanks the carcass some 4 metres away with the Bakaula male astride its rump: a remarkable feat, as sambar and tiger together must weigh about 400 kilogrammes. It exhausts her and she lets go of the throat. The male quickly pulls the carcass out of sight.

Laxmi strides off, entering a dry stream bed that leads to her den. She starts to call and is greeted by birdlike squeaks from her cubs. In minutes she returns with the cubs running round her in circles. One runs between her legs and tries to leap on her back. The other two are frisky and jump up the trunks of trees. They seem quite relaxed, as if this wasn't the first time they were going to share a feast with the Bakaula male. Soon they all disappear out of sight to where the male and the carcass lie. It is the second time in two days we have seen the resident male tiger in the role of father.

I believe that a tiger who has fathered a litter remains its protector, and that problems only arise when a new male usurps his range. Then the victorious male may kill his predecessor's

cubs in order to bring the adult females into oestrus again so that he can sire his own offspring. This practice is also known to happen among lions and primates. Sometimes a male tiger is killed and even eaten by the victor, but I have never come across this. However, I do know that a tigress once killed an adult male to protect her cubs. The male, who might have been an aggressive transient, was gnawed open and a chunk of his rump eaten.

After the age of six or seven months, the cubs are constantly on the prowl with their mother; they learn to stalk and hunt partridges, peacocks and hares. Their appetites increase and they devour ferociously whatever is presented to them. Their play becomes rougher as they charge, tumble and swat each other with their paws. This activity teaches them about hunting and defending themselves. One cub always emerges as the dominant member of a litter, eating first at a kill and behaving more boldly than his siblings. Although much of their diet is now meat, the cubs continue to suckle sporadically, but this seems to be mainly a means of maintaining close family bonds.

For their first year or so the cubs roam the forest with their mother, expanding their hunting range. In this way they learn the terrain, its landmarks and water-holes, the behaviour of prey and their mother's hunting techniques – lessons that will determine their future survival. A tigress facilitates the learning process by laming prey so that her cubs can bring it down and kill it. If a mother manages to rear her whole litter – normally from two to four cubs – to this age she is doing well. It is estimated that about 50 per cent of cubs do not survive their first year.

By the time the cubs are about fourteen months, close physical contact with their mother is no longer crucial. However, bonds of affection remain, as my notes reveal:

One warm day in March I arrived at the Semli water-hole to find three cubs resting in the cool of the undergrowth. The female cub moved towards us as we arrived, walking very close to the jeep. There was no sign of Laxmi. The cubs lazed around for nearly an hour and at four o'clock one of them suddenly became alert. It darted off to the far side, followed by its siblings. The forest exploded with the sound of purring as the cubs joyfully welcomed their mother: Laxmi had returned. We followed to find the cubs rubbing their flanks against Laxmi. All four tigers purred incessantly as the cubs licked, nuzzled and cuddled their mother.

With a tight grip on the folds of skin around the neck of the tigress, the tiger mates.
Mating takes place several times an hour, amidst growls, snarls and an orchestra of tiger sounds.

The last months before independence are spent in honing hunting skills. During this time the sub-adults are spray-marking, checking their territorial behaviour and getting ready to leave their mother. They are now able to kill peacocks, chital fawns and even the occasional langur by themselves. In fact, young tigers have been known to chase up trees in their search for this monkey! Adept as they are, it will take the cubs another year of effort to perfect their hunting techniques.

Tiger cubs spend nearly twenty months in close contact with their mother, but the time may vary depending on the nature and individual characteristics of each cub. The dominant cub is the first to leave. The young adults must now try to stake out a territory of their own in order to breed. For both sexes this usually means ousting a local resident, and fierce clashes, especially between males, do occur. In areas where prey is abundant, females occupy a range of about 10–15 square kilometres and the territory of the resident male will overlap that of two or three females. For the most part adult tigers avoid each other, marking their territory with scent, urine and scrapes on the ground. Any 'tiger area' is also likely to have its share of transients: males or females who have not yet managed to lay claim to a territory, or who have been banished from their own.

It may take a young tiger some years to establish him or herself in a territory, but if they are successful females are mature enough to breed at the age of three or four years, and males at five or six. It seems to be more difficult for a male to maintain his hold on a territory – perhaps simply because he is trying to cover a larger area: he is likely to be overthrown after about three or four years, while a breeding female may remain in the same territory for much longer. With a comparatively short gestation period of about 105 days, females can produce a litter every three years or so. But there are also times when females do not conceive – I have known a tigress who did not have a litter for seven years.

I believe the ages at which cubs leave their mother is also affected by the ecological system in which they live. Contrary to received wisdom about the tiger's solitary nature, I think tigers were forced into solitary and nocturnal lives as a result of persecution or habitat destruction by man, leading to shortage of prey. In effectively protected habitats, tigers may form temporary groups in order to hunt and share food. In Ranthambhore during the 1980s the tigers were largely undisturbed; they flourished and revealed facets of their family life that I would not have imagined possible.

A tiger rises aggressively on two feet to fight a rival. Sometimes they launch into a 'boxing match' as they swat one another's face.

The descendants of Hanuman

Let us now enter the world of the Hanuman langur, who is a constant presence in the tiger's forest. The langur is probably a source of great annoyance to the tiger, since it has remarkable eyesight and from its high perch it can spot the slightest movement; its shrill alarm call effectively warns all the other animals of danger.

Its ability to cover large distances on the ground has made the Hanuman langur one of the most widespread species of primate on the subcontinent. It ranges from altitudes of nearly 5000 metres in the Himalayas down to sea level, and lives in diverse habitats, from moist montane forest to semi-desert and arid regions. Its name is derived from the Sanskrit word *langulin*, which means 'long tail'.

The langur is primarily a forest-dwelling primate and has been the subject of much research. Much of its time is spent sitting in trees, but in open country it seems to be quite happy on the ground. Nevertheless, it is never far from a tree in case danger threatens. Langurs are omnivorous and able to digest large quantities of mature leaves, but they also feed on new leaves, seeds, nuts, fruits, grain and much more. They tend to keep their distance from the equally widespread macaques, but on rare occasions the two species have been found feeding together. In Ranthambhore, for example, I have seen single macaques joining a troop of langurs, living with them and trying to dominate them.

Langur troops divide into two types: stable troops of both males and females, and all-male troops which contain from two to fifty adults, sub-adults and juvenile males. Male bands continually try to take over control of mixed troops. When successful, the dominant member of the male band evicts the other adult and sub-adult males, both the residents and those of his own group, and kills the unweaned infants. As with tigers, it is believed that this will bring the females into oestrus and enable the new resident male to mate and produce his own offspring. Dominant males normally remain in control of a mixed troop for two or three years before being usurped in their turn.

Females remain a part of the same troop for nearly twenty years, so a troop normally consists of one or more extended families of mothers, grandmothers, sisters and aunts. They enter their reproductive cycles in their third year and can give birth every two years thereafter. The gestation period is six to seven months and babies remain dependent on their mother's milk for eight months, which means that the mother has to spend much of her time eating in order to provide energy for herself and her baby. All the females

The langur, regarded as sacred by all Hindus. A favourite prey of the leopard,
it also falls victim to the tiger's pounce.

in a troop help to look after the young, but most of the 'babysitting' is done by young females who have not yet given birth themselves. These young females seem to be fascinated by newborn babies; giving them this responsibility is a way of preparing them for motherhood when their turn comes.

An abundance of snakes

The king cobra is found all across India, often in thick forests and in tea and coffee plantations up to 1200 metres above sea level. It is the largest poisonous snake in the world, one specimen having been recorded as 5.6 metres long. The king cobra can attack without provocation, rearing itself high off the ground to strike, pumping poison into its target – usually other snakes and monitor lizards – with a chewing motion of its jaws.

King cobras are territorial and feed only within their own territory, although this may be quite large and may include villages or other areas inhabited by humans. The courtship of the king cobra is intriguing to watch: the female raises her head and the male crawls over her body. He checks her receptivity with a head-butt; if she is ready she lifts her tail and mating takes place.

Unlike other snakes, the female king cobra exhibits a certain amount of parental care. She first builds a nest using the coils of her body to gather leaves into a pile. Then, after laying her eggs, she settles herself into a small compartment above the nest to guard them during the 70-odd days before they hatch.

Second only in impressiveness to the king cobra is the spectacled cobra, which is 1 metre long, smooth-scaled, with black eyes and a wide neck. Its body is covered with a speckled white or yellow pattern, with a dark neck-band and white or yellowish underside. It gets its name from the connected pair of rings on its hood, which resemble spectacles. This shy creature is found across India and up to an elevation of 4000 metres, preferring to live in rice-growing areas, which attract rats.

Just before the monsoon the female spectacled cobra lays between twelve and thirty eggs in a rat hole or termite mound and remains with them for nearly two months till they hatch. The young disperse in a few weeks and start on a diet of insects and frogs. As they grow they become able to kill and swallow monitor lizards almost twice their own length.

Although it is the king cobra who generally features in snake worship, he is only the most prominent of a hugely diverse group. There are some 2000 species of snake in the

The Indian python in the process of swallowing a hog deer. There have been occasions when a tiger will kill a python and snatch the deer to feast on.

world, of which over 200 are found in India. From deserts to seas, swamps to glaciers, farmlands to mountains, snakes are everywhere. They may be nocturnal or diurnal in habit, and their skin, dry and often glossy, enables them to move rapidly. They are most active during the rains.

Snakes have a remarkable capacity to store fat and can go without food for months, but poisonous snakes usually eat once every few days, killing frogs, fish, lizards and insects by injecting them with venom. Some, such as the aptly named rat snake, are specialist feeders. Unlike the king cobra, which actively seeks out its prey, many vipers wait in ambush, strike out at their chosen victim, then follow its scent trail until it dies. Pythons, on the other hand, crush their prey and can kill animals as large as a small deer.

Most snakes mate once a year and incubate their eggs for sixty to eighty days. Young snakes grow fast and are forced to shed their skin once every couple of months. The lifespan of snakes in the wild is unknown, but pythons in captivity have been known to reach the age of twenty-two.

India's national bird

The alarm call of the peacock is a vital clue to the movement of predators, not least tigers and leopards. Young cubs often practise their hunting skills on peacocks. On one occasion in Ranthambhore a tiger was observed walking away with a peacock in its mouth, but the fan tail was covering its eyes, so that it kept bumping into trees and bushes.

Peacocks are found throughout the subcontinent, from the Himalayas to Sri Lanka, in scrubland or forest; they have been observed at altitudes of 1800 metres. They are normally seen in small groups, either all the same sex or one male with four or five females. Despite their flamboyant appearance they are naturally shy birds, slinking away into the undergrowth when disturbed but rarely taking to flight except to overcome an obstacle such as a river bed.

The peacock is a great harbinger of the approaching monsoon: his spectacular mating dance is seen all over the country just before the onset of the rains. This apparent ability to foretell the coming of rain has led popular belief to associate the peacock with fertility. Mating itself has rarely been observed: folklore suggests that the peacock drops a jewel from his beak and that the peahen picks it up and procreates!

Peacocks become very active and shrill as the time for mating approaches. If two cocks meet on the same territory, they turn on each other, lashing out with their feet in order to scare off their opponent. When a female enters the arena, the male bobs his neck up and down and rushes around her, finishing with a courtship dance that flashes the hundreds of 'eyes' in his feathers. In a nest hollowed out of the ground and lined

The peacock is India's national bird and protected throughout the country.
Young tigers learn to stalk and hunt by chasing peafowl.

with a few twigs and leaves the peahen produces a single brood of two to six chicks every year during the monsoon. The male plays no part in incubating the eggs or looking after the young.

At dusk in Ranthambhore peacocks enact the same ritual every evening: they line up on the walls of the fort which stands on a cliff above the park and, after much calling, descend to specific roosting trees for the night. I never tire of watching them.

Giant vegetarians

Some of the finest elephant habitats are in the national parks of Corbett, Nagarahole, Mudumalai, Bandipur, Periyar and the *terai* belt in the foothills of the Himalayas. They are also found in parts of Bihar, Orissa and West Bengal, as well as the northeastern and southwestern tracts of deciduous, evergreen and tropical rainforest in Karnataka, Kerala and Tamil Nadu. The elephant shares many of these places with the tiger, and I believe the fates of both species are deeply entwined.

Current estimates suggest that 20,000–25,000 elephants roam the Indian forests in their constant quest for food. They are also found in the Sri Lankan forests, where thirty years ago poaching had reduced their numbers so drastically that they were regarded as endangered. Thanks to strict enforcement of anti-poaching laws their numbers are now on the increase, but even so a big male with splendid ivory tusks is a rare sight.

Elephants' vegetarian diet is diverse and includes grasses, bamboos, legumes, the bark of certain plants and trees, and succulent climbers, creepers and palms. The leaves of fig trees and fruits, such as tamarind, wood apple and mango, are all seasonal delicacies that form a vital part of their menu. Their fruit-eating habits also help to disperse seeds and ensure the regeneration of these species.

The Asian elephant was originally found across western, southern and Southeast Asia, including the islands of Sri Lanka, Java, Sumatra and Borneo, and into China, but today it has gone from western Asia, Java and most of China. Early written records about the capture and training of elephants appear in the Rig-Veda hymns (c. 2000 BC) and the Upanishad treatises (800–500 BC), but the earliest depictions appear on cave walls in Pachmari, Madhya Pradesh, which date back 10,000 years. Elephants have long been used for military purposes, and the seventeenth-century Mogul emperor Jehangir is supposed to have had 12,000 of them in his army.

Mahouts, or elephant men, use domesticated elephants for a variety of purposes – viewing wildlife, patrolling conservation areas or for forestry operations. In parts of Assam potential working elephants are captured at the age of five or six and tied down for weeks in the early stages of domestication. The largest land mammal goes through unimaginable trauma as it is tamed at the hands of man. During this time, elephants learn to respond to human commands and often develop a close and loyal relationship with their keeper. This remarkable relationship is celebrated throughout the year when the best elephants are selected to participate in temple rituals that were established over 200 years ago.

Sitting on a domesticated elephant and watching wild ones is a fascinating experience. From this vantage point I once watched the elephant I was riding sniff out a tiger's trail, then come to a restless halt and lift its trunk in warning. There, under a tree, sat two sub-adult tigers watching us closely. Too young to pose a real threat, they ran off to the shelter of a bush when the elephant trumpeted, but returned to watch when their curiosity got the better of them.

Indian elephants live in a basic family unit consisting of an adult cow and her off-spring; the daughters will be of all ages, but the sons remain with their mothers only until puberty. This family unit belongs to an extended family, which may include two

In this land of elephants reverence for Lord Ganesha is a part of everyday life for most Indians. People's tolerance for elephants, even when they go on the rampage, is legendary.

or more adult cows and their offspring. Males disperse at puberty normally to form 'bull groups', but they may also remain solitary; in either case they associate with a family when a cow is in oestrus.

An elephant family's home range fluctuates, depending on the season and availability of food, but 100–1000 square kilometres is average. Within this range an elephant can consume up to 1.9 per cent of its body weight (135–300 kilogrammes) in just twelve hours of feeding. It will also consume 100 litres of water at a time, drinking 200–500 litres a day depending on the season and temperature.

Almost all mature bull elephants can go into an annual period of heightened excitement and aggression known as musth, when a pungent-smelling fluid is discharged from the temporal glands between the eyes and ears. During this time bulls search for oestrus cows and compete ferociously with other bulls for their favours. Battles between two of these giants make the earth shake and may go on for many days, resulting in serious wounds and even death for the loser. After successful mating, there is a gestation period of nineteen to twenty-two months.

Bonds between adult cow and offspring are strong. Communication is achieved through scent, touch, sound and body language, involving much rubbing, pressing and entwining. Aunts and older siblings also keep a watchful eye on the young and participate in their care. Danger is communicated by sound, but at frequencies that may not be audible to humans. Any threat to one of its number results in the entire herd rushing to its defence. When protecting their young, the herd bunches together like a phalanx, keeping the calves at the rear between a group of cows. Those at the front then wheel around and attack the intruder. Despite this, experienced tigers still manage to penetrate the protective net of adults and kill the calves. Human intrusion is also feared, and the slightest whiff of it is enough to put a herd on high alert.

Without doubt, elephants have a long and accurate memory, which is combined with a remarkable sensitivity. Their reaction to discovering elephant bones, for instance, is to pile leaves and mud over them, as if conducting a burial. Similarly, adult cows have sat by their dead calves for many days, refusing to leave them.

This giant herbivore is sensitive in more than thought and emotion. Its massive and prehistoric-looking trunk has a tip that is able to explore the ground with astonishing delicacy. Its sensitivity can also be a drawback, however, because a bite from a venomous snake can be lethal, particularly to calves.

The elephant's trunk is multi-functional, used for breathing, sucking, blowing, trumpeting and smelling. It can also be used like a hand, tearing up grass and pounding dirt from it, selecting fruits, picking tiny flowers or carrying huge logs of wood. The trunk can act as a weapon or be used to express emotion – it may be coiled protectively around a calf or used to caress other elephants. Young bulls use their trunks to pluck branches and leaves, and use their body weight to push down trees. This last habit, once believed to be needlessly destructive, is actually beneficial because the fallen trees provide a micro-habitat for small creatures and the gaps allow for new and vigorous regeneration. Similarly, the elephant's dramatic clearance of thick vegetation allows smaller herbivores to find new feeding grounds after its departure.

Though the adults are too large to be vulnerable to natural predators, elephants are at the mercy of human beings: plundering plants, manipulating habitats, shifting cultivation, creating dams and hydro-electric projects, grazing cattle, starting fires, altering the landscape and, not least, poaching, all take a heavy toll on elephant populations. Every year across the world thousands of elephants are killed for their ivory tusks, and this has left many areas short of mature bulls. The rapaciousness of human beings has left the subcontinent with seriously fragmented habitats, so elephants are often forced to search for new feeding grounds, which can take them into farmland or villages and lead to clashes with humans.

The elephant's continued survival, despite poaching, is largely thanks to the protection it commands because of its association with Ganesha, the elephant-headed son of Siva. But for how long will that continue?

What of the future?

India is a land where man and nature have enjoyed a harmony seldom seen elsewhere in the world. Sadly, that relationship is now breaking down and some of the connections seem fated to be lost forever. The delicate fabric of myth, legend and religious belief, woven together by centuries of experience and wisdom, has been smashed apart in the last decade by alien cultures and the power of the electronic media. India and its neighbouring countries have entered the ugly world of consumerism and the free-market economy. Traditional values are vanishing as people pursue their new god, easy money. Habitats are gobbled up under the guise of 'development' and animals are killed for the cash they fetch. Sacred trees are being pulverized under the pressures of greed. Respect for nature, a cornerstone of life throughout the subcontinent for thousands of years, is fast disappearing. Economic forces have engulfed life and broken away the deep-rooted links between man and nature. A looming crisis threatens to wipe out the natural heritage of India.

OVERLEAF *A tigress if disturbed when she has newly born cubs will change her den, and each cub will be carefully carried to the new location.*

Epilogue

Our journey has ended and we have explored the rich fragments that remain of the Indian subcontinent's natural heritage. Nearly 1.3 billion people share this land of the tiger, and the population increases by 2 per cent every year. Changing economic policies, the spread of television and a consequent demand for new-fangled products have had near-fatal impacts on our natural resources. People exploit, loot and pillage the wilderness under the guise of development and livelihood rights, a systematic dismantling of nature which I, as an observer, regard as the most tragic experience of my life. The land of the tiger is being torn apart.

The tiger is a potent symbol of India's natural heritage and an excellent indicator of its health. Sadly, the indications are bad. Loss of habitat and indiscriminate poaching mean that hundreds of tigers have vanished each year, and with them thousands of other animals slaughtered for their bones, fur, claws or anything else we humans desire.

Politicians and administrators on the subcontinent have failed its wildlife, and the absence of political concern suggests that some of the breathtaking natural events described in this book will probably cease to exist before the end of the twentieth century. Will flamingoes continue to feast on baby shrimps in the hot salt-flats of the desert, or will the entire area be destroyed by salt extraction? Will the timber tycoons who have deforested most of the Himalayan forests now turn to the few protected fragments that remain? Will the magnificent mangrove swamps of the Sundarbans turn into shrimp factories to feed the growing demands of the East? Will World Heritage sites, such as Bharatpur and Manas, be ripped apart by poachers, insurgents and 'developmental' needs? Will the future of the subcontinent be relegated to a handful of national parks?

Some of these tragedies have already begun, and many others are possible. The solutions in today's world are few and far-between. They rest in the hands of people – people who care for the wild, for nature, for the right to life of all nature's creations.

One of the largest tuskers to be found on the subcontinent. This elephant
lives in Sri Lanka and is worshipped by hundreds of thousands of people each year.
As forests vanish, the future of the Asiatic elephant remains a big question mark.
Here today, gone tomorrow?

Forest guards holding the skin of a poached tiger in Pench reserve in Madhya Pradesh.

If the people who care are able to translate their will into the tangible protection of nature, we have a ray of hope. A new ideology must be created – a way of life that is entwined with consideration for the wilderness and not with economic models of growth.

I am continuing to search for this new ideology. Let those of us who care engage in battle together to ensure the survival of some of the Earth's great natural spectacles, even if it takes another century.

The future of the human race is inextricably bound up with the fate of the tiger and all the countless living organisms that form the fabric of life on this planet. Saving the land of the tiger means starting from scratch in village, town and city, creating political will through the power of the people, ensuring better legislation that protects the right of wildlife to live, and enforcing the laws of the land to prevent large-scale violations of the fabric of nature. This enormous challenge requires courage from each and every one of us – the courage to move away from insular lives around television sets and to enter the public arena of battle.

But we must do it fast. There is little time left. If we don't, future generations will never forgive us for the crimes we allowed to be perpetrated in the name of development and economics. The roots that bind people and nature together have been trampled and weakened, but they can be revitalized if we work together. The Earth, from which we were all born, will repay us many times over.

1998 is the Year of the Tiger in the Chinese calendar. Can it survive the pressure it faces?

BIBLIOGRAPHY

Abbreviations used for publishers are:
BNHS Bombay Natural History Society
IUCN International Union for the Conservation
 of Nature
JBNHS Journal of the Bombay Natural History
 Society
NBT National Book Trust
OUP Oxford University Press
WWF World Wide Fund for Nature
ZSI Zoological Survey of India

GENERAL

Ahmad, Yusuf S., *With the Wild Animals of Bengal*,
 Dhaka, Y.S. Ahmad, 1981
Alfred, J.R.B. et al., *The Red Data Book of Indian
 Animals, Part 1: Vertebrata*, Calcutta, ZSI, 1994
Ali, Salim, *The Mohgal Emperors of India as Naturalists
 and Sportsmen*, Bombay, JBNHS 31(4) 833-61
Allen, Dr Gerald R. and Steene, Roger, *Indo-Pacific
 Coral Reef Field Guide*, Singapore, 1994
Alvi, M.A. and Rhaman, A., *Jahangir – The Naturalist*,
 Delhi, 1968
de Alwis, Lyn, *National Parks of Ceylon*,
 Colombo, 1969
Bedi, Rajesh and Bedi, Ramesh, *Indian Wildlife*,
 New Delhi, Brijbasi, 1984;
 Wild India, New Delhi, Brijbasi, 1990
Bonner, Nigel, *Whales of the World*, London,
 Blandford, 1989
Brandar, A. Dunbar, *Wild Animals of Central India*,
 London, Arnold, 1923
Breeden, Stanley and Wright, Belinda,
 *Through The Tiger's Eyes: Chronicle of India's
 Vanishing Wildlife*, USA, Ten Speed Press, 1997
Champion, F., *In Sunlight and Shadow*, London,
 Chatto & Windus, 1925;
 With a Camera in Tiger Land, London,
 Chatto & Windus, 1927
Corbet, G.B. and Hill, J.E., *The Mammals of the
 Indomalayan Region*, London/Oxford, Natural
 History Museum/OUP, 1992

Cronin, E.W., *The Arun: a Natural History
 of the World's Deepest Valley*, Boston,
 Houghton Mifflin, 1979
Cubitt, Gerald and Mountfort, Guy, *Wild India*,
 London, Collins, 1985
Daniel, J.C., *A Century of Natural History*, Bombay,
 BNHS/OUP, 1986;
 A Week with Elephants, Bombay, BNHS, 1996;
 The Leopard in India – A Natural History,
 Dehra Dun, Natraj, 1996
Divyabhanusinh, *The End of a Trail; The Cheetah
 in India*, New Delhi, Banyan Books, 1996
Eisenberg, John F., McKay, George and
 Seidensticker, John, *Asian Elephants – Studies
 in Sri Lanka*, Washington, Smithsonian, 1990
Flemming, Robert L. Jr., *The Ecology, Flora and Fauna
 of Midland Nepal*, Kathmandu, Tribhuvan
 University, 1977
Gee, E.P., *The Wildlife of India*, London, Collins, 1964
Ghorpade, M.Y., *Sunlight and Shadows*, London,
 Gollancz, 1983
Green, M.J.B., *IUCN Directory of South Asian Protected
 Areas*, Cambridge, IUCN, 1990;
 *Nature Reserves of the Himalaya and the Mountains
 of Central Asia*, New Delhi, OUP, 1993
Gurung, K.K., *Heart of the Jungle; the Wildlife of
 Chitwan, Nepal*, London, Andre Deutsch, 1983;
 *Mammals of the Indian Sub-continent and where
 to watch them*, Oxford, Indian Experience, 1996
Hardy, Sarah B., *The Langurs of Abu*, Cambridge, USA,
 Harvard University Press, 1977
Hillard, Darla, *Vanishing Tracks – Four Years Among the
 Snow Leopards of Nepal*, London, ElmTree, 1989
Hooker, J.D., *Himalayan Journals,* 2 vols, London, John
 Murray, 1855
Insight Guide to Indian Wildlife, Singapore, Apa
 Publications, 1992
Insight Guide to Sri Lanka, Singapore, Apa
 Publications, 1995
Israel, S. and Sinclair, Toby, *Indian Wildlife*, Singapore,
 Apa Publications, 1987
Jefferies, Margaret, *Sagarmatha, The Story of Mount
 Everest National Park*, Auckland, 1986

Khan, M.A.R., *Mammals of Bangladesh*, Dhaka,
  Nazima Reza, 1985
Krishnan, M., *India's Wildlife 1959-70*, Bombay,
  BNHS, 1975;
  The Handbook of India's Wildlife, Madras, TTK, 1983
Manfredi, Paola, *In Danger*, New Delhi,
  Ranthambhore Foundation, 1997
Mattiessen, Peter, *The Snow Leopard*, London,
  Chatto & Windus, 1979
Mishra, Hemanta and Mierow, Dorothy,
  Wild Animals of Nepal, Kathmandu, 1976;
  and Jefferies, M., *Royal Chitwan National Park;*
  Wildlife Heritage of Nepal, Seattle,
  The Mountaineers, 1991
Mukherjee, Ajit, *Extinct and Vanishing Birds and*
  Mammals of India, Calcutta, Indian Museum,
  1966
Oliver, William, *The Pigmy Hog*, Jersey,
  Jersey Wildlife Preservation Trust, 1980
Owen Edmunds, Tom, *Bhutan*, Elm Tree Books, 1989
Panwar, H.S., *Kanha National Park – A Handbook*,
  Ahmadabad, CEE, 1991
Philips, W.W., *A Manual of the Mammals of Sri Lanka,*
  Parts 1-3, Colombo, 1980-84
Prater, S., *The Book of Indian Animals*, Bombay,
  BNHS, 1988
Ranjitsinh, M.K., *The Indian Blackbuck*, Dehra Dun,
  Natraj, 1990;
  Beyond the Tiger, Portraits of South Asian Wildlife,
  New Delhi, Brijbasi, 1997
Roberts, T.J., *The Mammals of Pakistan*, London,
  Benn, 1977
Roonwul, M.L. and Mohnot, S.M., *The Primates of*
  South Asia, Cambridge, USA, Harvard University
  Press, 1977
Saharia, V.B., *Wildlife in India*, Dehra Dun,
  Natraj, 1982
Sanderson, G.P., *Thirteen Years among the Wild Beasts*
  of India, London, W.H. Allen, 1896
Schaller, G.B., *The Deer and the Tiger; A Study of*
  Wildlife in India, Chicago, Chicago University
  Press, 1969;
  Mountain Monarchs; Wild Sheep and Goats of the
  Himalaya, Chicago, Chicago University Press, 1977
  Stones of Silence; Journeys in the Himalaya, London,
  Andre Deutsch, 1980
Shahi, S.P., *Backs to the Wall; Saga of Wildlife in Bihar,*
  Delhi, Affiliated East-West Press, 1977
Sharma, B.D., *High Altitude Wildlife in India,*
  New Delhi, Oxford & India Book House, 1994
Sheshadri, B., *The Twilight of India's Wildlife*, London,
  John Baker, 1969;

India's Wildlife and Reserves, New Delhi,
  Sterling, 1986
Sukumar, R., *The Asian Elephant*, Cambridge,
  Cambridge University Press, 1989;
  Elephant Days and Nights, New Delhi, OUP, 1994
Tikader, B.K., *Threatened Animals of India*, Calcutta,
  ZSI, 1993
Tyabji, Hashim, *Bandhavgarh National Park,*
  New Delhi, 1994

TIGERS

Barnes, Simon, *Tiger*, London, Boxtree, 1994
Chakrabarti, Kalyan, *Man-eating Tigers*, Calcutta,
  Darbari Prokashan, 1992
Courtney, Nicholas, *The Tiger – Symbol of Freedom*,
  London, Quartet Books, 1980
Denzau, Gertrude and Helmut, *Königstiger,* Steinfurt,
  Tecklenborg Verlag, 1996
Desai, J.H. and Malhotra, A.K., *The White Tiger,*
  New Delhi, Publications Division, Ministry
  of Information & Broadcasting, 1992
Fend, Werner, *Die Tiger Von Abutschmar,*
  Vienna, Verlag Fritz Molden, 1972
Ives, Richard, *Of Tigers and Men*, New York,
  Doubleday, 1995
Jackson, Peter. *Endangered Species – Tigers*, London,
  The Apple Press, 1990
McDougal, Charles, *Face of the Tiger*, London,
  Andre Deutsch and Rivington, 1977
McNeely, Jeffrey A. and Wachtel, P.S., *The Soul*
  of the Tiger, New York, Doubleday, 1988
Meacham, Cory, *How the Tiger Lost Its Stripes,*
  New York, Harcourt Brace, 1997
Montgomery, Sy, *Spell of the Tiger*, Boston,
  Houghton Mifflin, 1995
Mountfort, Guy, *Tigers,* Newton Abbot,
  David & Charles, 1973;
  Saving the Tiger, London, Michael Joseph, 1981
Niyogi, Tushar K., *Tiger Cult of the Sundarbans,*
  Calcutta, Anthropological Survey of India, 1996
Perry, Richard, *The World of the Tiger*, London,
  Cassell, 1964
Sankhala, Kailash, *Tigerland*, Bobbs, Merrill, 1975
Sankhala, Kailash, *Return of the Tiger*, New Delhi,
  Lustre Press, 1993;
  Tiger, London, Collins, 1978
Schaller, George B., *The Deer and the Tiger*, Chicago,
  University of Chicago Press, 1967
Seidensticker, John, *Tigers*, Stillwater, USA,
  Voyageur Press, 1986
Server, Lee, *Tigers*, New York, Todtri, 1991

Shah, Anup and Manoj, *A Tiger's Tale*,
Kingston-upon-Thames, Fountain Press, 1996
Singh, Arjan, *Tiger Haven*, London, Macmillan, 1973;
Tara – A Tigress, London, Quartet Books, 1981;
The Legend of the Man Eater, New Delhi,
Ravidayal,1993;
Tiger Tiger, London, Jonathan Cape, 1984
Stracey, P.D., *Tigers*, London, Arthur Barker Ltd, 1968
Sunquist, Fiona, and Sunquist, Mel, *Tiger Moon*,
Chicago, The University of Chicago Press, 1988
Thapar, Valmik, *The Tiger's Destiny*, London,
Kyle Cathie, 1992;
The Secret Life, London, Hamish Hamilton, 1989;
Tiger – Portrait of a Predator, London, Collins, 1986;
With Tigers in the Wild, New Delhi, Vikas, 1982
Tilson, R.L. and Seal, V., *Tigers of the World*:
*The biology, bio politics, management and conservation
of an endangered species,* New Jersey,
Noyes Publications, 1987
Toovey, J., ed., *Tigers of the Raj*, Gloucester,
Alan Sutton, 1987
Ward, Geoffrey C., *Tiger-Wallahs*, New York,
Harper Collins, 1993
Zwaenepoel, Jean-Pierre, *Tigers*, San Francisco,
Chronicle Books, 1992

BIRDS

Ali, Salim, *The Book of Indian Birds*, Bombay, BNHS,
1941 and 1996;
Birds of Kerala, Bombay, OUP, 1986;
Birds of Kutch, Bombay, OUP, 1986;
Birds of Sikkim, Bombay, OUP, 1962;
Indian Hill Birds, Bombay, OUP, 1949 and 1979;
Bird Study in India; its History and Importance,
New Delhi, Indian Council for Cultural
Relations, 1979;
The Fall of a Sparrow, Bombay, OUP, 1984;
Field Guide to the Birds of the Eastern Himalayas,
Bombay, OUP, 1977
Ali, S. and Piley, Dillon S., *The Handbook of the Birds of
India and Pakistan,* 10 vols, Bombay, OUP, 1968-74
Baker, E.C. Stuart, *Fauna/Birds of British India,*
8 vols, London, Taylor & Francis, 1928-30;
Indian Ducks and their Allies, Bombay, BNHS, 1908;
Indian Pigeons and Doves, Bombay, BNHS, 1913;
The Gamebirds of India, Burma and Ceylon, 3 vols,
Bombay, BNHS, 1921
Beebe, William, *Pheasant Jungles*, Lower Basildon,
World Pheasant Association, 1994
Choudhury, Anwaruddin, *Checklist of the Birds
of Assam*, Guwahati, Sophia Press, 1990

Daniels, R.J., *A Field Guide to the Birds of
Southwestern India*, New Delhi, OUP, 1997
Dharamkumarsinhji, R.S., *The Birds of Saurashtra*,
Bombay, 1957
Dick, John Henry, *A Pictorial Guide to the Birds of the
Indian Sub-continent*, Bombay, OUP/BNHS, 1983
Ewans, Martin, *Bharatpur – Bird Paradise*, London,
H.F. & G. Witherby, 1989
Fleming, R.L. Snr. and Jnr, and Bangdel, J., *Birds
of Nepal*, Kathmandu, 1976
Ganguli, Usha, *A Guide to the Birds of the Delhi Area*,
New Delhi, Indian Council for Agricultural
Research, 1975
Grewal, Bikram with Wright, Gillian and Monga, S.,
Birds of the Indian Subcontinent, Hong Kong,
Odyssey, 1993
Henry, G.M., *A Guide to the Birds of Ceylon*, OUP,
1955 and 1971
Inskipp, Carol, *A Birdwatchers' Guide to Nepal*,
Huntingdon, Prion, 1988;
Nepal's Forest Birds, their status and conservation,
Cambridge, International Council for Bird
Preservation, 1989;
*The Birds and Mammals of the Annapurna
Conservation Area*, Kathmandu, Annapurna
Conservation Area Project, 1989
Inskipp, Carol and Tim, *A Guide to the Birds of Nepal*,
London, Christopher Helm, 1985 and 2nd ed.
1992;
An Introduction to Birdwatching in Bhutan, Thimpu,
WWF, 1995
Inskipp, Carol and Cocker, P.M., *A Himalayan
Ornithologist: The Life and Work of Brian Hodgson*,
London, OUP, 1989
Inskipp, Tim et al., *An Annotated Checklist of the Birds
of the Oriental Region*, Sandy, Bedfordshire, Oriental
Bird Club, 1996
Jerdon, T.C., *The Birds of India*, 3 vols, 1862-64
Kalpavriksh, *What's the Bird?,* New Delhi,
Kalpavriksh, 1991
Kotagama, Sarath and Prithviraj, Fernando, *A Field
Guide to the Birds of Sri Lanka*, Colombo, 1994
MacDonald, Malcolm, *Birds in My Indian Garden*,
London, Jonathan Cape, 1960
Phillips, W.W.A., *Birds of Ceylon,* 4 vols, Colombo,
Ceylon Daily News, 1949-61
Ripley, S. Dillon, *Search for the Spiny Babbler*, Boston,
Houghton Mifflin, 1952;
A Synopsis of the Birds of India and Pakistan,
Bombay, BNHS, 1961, and revised 1982
Robert, T., *The Birds of Pakistan,* 2 vols, Karachi,
OUP, 1991 and 1992

Sankahala, Kailash, *Gardens of Eden: the Waterbird Sanctuary at Bharatpur*, New Delhi, Vikas, 1990

Tikader, B.K., *Birds of the Andaman and Nicobar Islands*, Calcutta, ZSI, 1984

Whistler, Hugh, *The Popular Hand Book of Indian Birds*, London, Gurney & Jackson, 1928

World Atlas of Birds, London, Mitchell Beazley, 1974

Woodcock, Martin, *Handguide to the Birds of the Indian Sub-continent*, London, Collins, 1980

REPTILES AND AMPHIBIANS

Daniel, J.C., *Field Guide to the Amphibians of Western India*, Bombay, BNHS, 1963, 1975 and 1989;
The Book Of Indian Reptiles, Bombay, BNHS, 1983;

Das, Indraneil, *Colour Guide to the Turtles and Tortoises of the Indian Sub-continent*, R & A Publishing, 1991;
Turtles and Tortoises of India, Bombay, OUP/WWF, 1965

Deoras, P.J., *Snakes of India*, New Delhi, NBT, 1965

Deuti, Kaushik and Goswami, B.C. Bharati, *Amphibians of West Bengal Plains,* Calcutta, WWF, 1995

Fleming, R.L. Sr. and Jr, *Some Snakes from Nepal*, Bombay, BNHS, 1974

Ghorpurey, K.G., *Snakes of India*, Bombay, 1937

Smith, M.A., *Fauna of British India; Reptiles and Amphibia,* 3 vols, London, Taylor & Francis, 1931-43

Tikader, B. K. and Sharma R. C., *Handbook of Indian Testudines*, Calcutta, ZSI, 1985

Wall, Major F., *Poisonous Terrestrial Snakes of India*, New Delhi, Macmillan, 1978

Whitaker, Romulus, *Common Indian Snakes*, New Delhi, Macmillan, 1978

Whitaker, Rom and Zai and Das, Indraneil, *The World of Turtles and Crocodiles*, New Delhi, NBT, 1993

INSECTS AND SPIDERS

Antram, Chas B., *Butterflies of India*, Calcutta, Thacker, Spink and Co, 1924

Haribal, Meena, *The Butterflies of the Sikkim Himalayas*, Gangtok, SNCF, 1992

Mani, M. S., *Insects*, New Delhi, NBT, 1971;
Butterflies of the Himalaya, New Delhi, Oxford & India Book House, 1986

Pocock, R. I., *Fauna of British India; Arachnida*, London, Taylor & Francis, 1900

Smith, C., *Commoner Butterflies of Nepal*, Kathmandu, 1976;

The Butterflies Of Nepal, Kathmandu, 1988

Tikader, B. K., *Spiders*, New Delhi, NBT, 1980;
Handbook of Indian Spiders, Calcutta, ZSI, 1987

Vijayalakshmi, K. and Ahimaz, Preston, *Spiders: An Introduction*, Madras, Cre-A, 1993

Wynter-Blyth, M. A., *Butterflies of the Indian Region*, Bombay, BNHS, 1957

FLOWERS AND TREES

Ashton, M. et al., *A Field Guide to the Common Trees and Shrubs of Sri Lanka*, Colombo, WHTSL, 1997

Bharucha, F.R., *Plant Geography of India*, Delhi, OUP, 1983

Blatter, E.X., *Beautiful Flowers of Kashmir*, 2 vols., London, John Bale, Sons & Danielsson Ltd, 1928-29;
Palms of British India, London, OUP, 1926;
and Millard, Walter S., *Some Beautiful Indian Trees*, Bombay, BNHS, 1937 and 1977

Bole, P.V., and Vaghani, Yogini, *Field Guide to the Common Trees of India*, Bombay, OUP/WWF, 1986

Bor, N.L. and Raizada, M.B., *Some Beautiful Indian Climbers and Shrubs*, Bombay, BNHS, 1954 and 1982

Brandis, D., *Indian Trees*, London, Constable, 1906

Champion, F. and Seth, *The Forest Types of India*, Delhi, Govt of India, 1962

Desmond, Ray, *The European Discovery of the Indian Flora*, Oxford, OUP, 1992

Gupta, S.M., *Plant Myths and Traditions in India*, Leiden, E. Brill, 1971

Hooker, Joseph, *The Flora of British India,* 7 vols, London, L. Reeve, 1872-97

Kingdon-Ward, Frank, *Assam Adventure*, London, Cape, 1941;
The Land of the Blue Poppy, London, Cambridge University Press, 1913;
Plant Hunting on the Edge of the World, London, Gollancz, 1930;
Plant Hunter in Manipur, London, Cape, 1952

Mierow, M. and Shresthra, T.B., *Himalayan Flowers and Trees*, Kathmandu, 1978

Nasir, E. and Ali, S.I., *Flora of (West) Pakistan*, Karachi, 1970

Polunin, Oleg and Stainton, Adam, *Flowers of the Himalaya*, Oxford, OUP, 1984

Santapau, H., *Common Trees*, New Delhi, NBT, 1966

Stainton, Adam, *Forests of Nepal*, London, John Murray, 1972

Stewart, R.R., *Flora of Ladakh*, Calcutta, 1916

INDEX

PICTURE CREDITS

For more information on saving the Land of the Tiger write to:

Valmik Thapar

TIGER LINK

19 Kautilya Marg

New Delhi 110021

India